Education, Knowledge and the Computer

Kenneth V. Lorimer, M.Phil., PhD.

Link-Frame Publishing International
P.O. Box 26265
San Diego, CA 92196-0265

STUDIES IN EDUCATION, KNOWLEDGE AND INTELLIGENT COMPUTER SYSTEMS

Education, Knowledge and the Computer
by Kenneth V. Lorimer

Contents

Chapter   *Page*

1   **Knowledge, Information Technology and**

*What is Information? Information Workers; Know-
ledge, Technology and Development; Human
Capital; The Knowledge Industry: The Value of
Knowledge; Social and Political Value, Qualita-
tive Values and Opportunity Costs; The Nature of
Knowledge; The Seeds of Information Technology
and Intelligent Computer Systems; Colleges and
Universities as Key Institutions for the Creation of
21st Century Society. Questions for Discussion and
Review.*

2   **How Data is Represented Internally in**

*Data and the Development of the Computer.
Why Mathematical Number Systems are
Important to Understanding Computers; Bits and
Bytes; Bits and Word Size; Binary and Decimal
Number Systems; The Octal Number System; the
Hexadecimal Number System; Codes; Machine
Language; Assembler Language. Questions for
Discussion and Review.*

3

*Definitions: Algorithm and Program; Criteria for
Algorithm; Steps in Program Development; How*

Preface

The book, *Education, Knowledge and The Computer*, relies on an interdisciplinary approach to some common issues involving five well-recognized disciplines: education, philosophy, mathematics, computer science, and social science. Issues in education and knowledge have been raised and hotly debated by such eminent educators as Hirst, P.H., and Peters, R.S., and philosophers like Bertrand Russell, A.N. Whitehead, Jerome Bruner and others over last fifty years, and perhaps even earlier. But what is different today, is the predominance of computers and developments in artificial intelligence involving the design of computer programs containing knowledge that emulates the reasoning process of human experts in a particular domain.

The modern computer also is used as an aid to instruction, and as a tool for knowledge processing. The role of knowledge in social systems, and as a product of development also has taken on a new light which hitherto was not recognized as an important economic factor.

Knowledge of computers and an understanding of the role of computers in education are very important, particularly at a time when the amount of time and money spent in these areas are increasing. If not clearly defined, lots of resources can be wasted on projects earmarked for education, though not logically or conceptually connected with education.

Except for a required elementary mathematical knowledge, no other prerequisites, nor preliminary knowledge of computers are needed to understand this book. Technical terms are clearly defined and the text is presented in a simple and progressive way. Questions for Discussion and Review following each Chapter are included to provide in class activities, provoke thought, and to test and reinforce your understanding the topics covered.

KENNETH V. LORIMER

CALIFORNIA, U.S.A.
June, 1995

Acknowledgement

This book is dedicated to perseverance

I wish to acknowledge my indebtedness to Professor Frank George, Professor Gordon Pask, and Dr. Mike Elstob at the Department of Cybernetics in the School of Engineering at Brunel University for providing a rich learning environment while attending that institution as a graduate student and research scholar, some years ago. While insisting on "rigor," these "teachers" and others provided the opportunity for me to attend and participate in many joint-colloquia where scholars from different disciplines, research centers, and financially oriented people openly discussed their views on important problems with sometimes heated difference of opinion and presented their solution for discussion. The success of these joint meetings and colloquia gave graduate students and participants an opportunity to acquire valuable knowledge, develop judgements, sharpen their skills in analyzing problems, and develop an appreciation for an interdisciplinary approach to some common problems and issues.

Also, I was greatly encouraged by Mr. A.G. Donald and Professor Stafford Beer, during my years as a graduate student. I am indebted to these educators.

I like to mention my mother, other relatives and some close friends who have played a positive role in my life. Also, special thanks to Mr. Monroe Ahrenstein and other colleagues for reading the early draft of this book and for their comments.

Finally, I must express my gratitude to my wife, Tina for typing the manuscripts during the long-drawn-out write and rewriting of this book.

About the Author

Kenneth V. Lorimer is an International consultant and author in Education, Knowledge and the Computer. He received a M.Phil. and a PhD. in Cybernetics and Information Systems in the School of Engineering from Brunel University, Uxbridge, England.

Dr. Lorimer was consultant to the famous PLATO System, a multimedia computer-based educational delivery system.

He has been involved in applying Cybernetic, and Artificial Intelligence techniques, and technology to teaching and education. Dr. Lorimer also is an expert in designing information system for planning and control (including cost and management systems and of network systems).

Dr. Lorimer has over two decades of experience, holding both teaching and management positions. He is President and head of the Cybernetics and Information Technology Center, and was Senior Lecturer, Visiting Professor and Professor at several major Polytechnics and Universities in England, Canada and the United States of America.

Dr. Lorimer is the Author of many technical papers, articles, instructional manuals and monographs. He also is a member of several professional associations.

Besides his scholarly and professional activities, he practices Kendo, the Art and Philosophy of Japanese Fencing, and holds the rank of *Godon* (5 Dan) in Kendo.

Chapter 1 ‖ Knowledge, Information Technology and Economic Development

Knowledge and Information technology are emerging topics of interest for economics, management, education, and computer science. There are many reasons for this emerging interest. First, in the developed nations of United States of America and Western Europe, there has been a dramatic increase in the number of people engaged in the information and knowledge processing industry. Second, when you study the employment structure of these developed nations within the last thirty years, you will observe that the amount of energy expended in manufacturing in both machine hours and person-hours is less than what it used to be thirty years ago. This change alters the structure of employment and the nature of economic activity by having less of the gross national product coming from manufacturing and more from "brain" and knowledge processing. A reason for this change is due in part to a response to the growing strength of industrial and commercial competition from other nations.

And third, there is a realization that the transfer of knowledge processing and information technology from research departments and defence agencies to the civilian economy of a nation can be an important stimulus to economic growth.

All three of these developments owe their ascendancy to knowledge and the computer. The computer is an electronic machine that accepts *data* in a prescribed form, processes the data and supplies the results of the processing in a specified format as *information*, or *knowledge* or as signals to control automatically some further machine or process. This definition covers three main types of computers: *digital computers, analog computers,* and *hybrid computers.*

Types of Computers

An *analog* computer is a computer that uses analog representation of the data. It does not use binary digits as in the digital computer. Instead, it measures continuous physical or electrical quantities such as pressure, temperature, currents, voltage, length or shaft rotation. Analog computers are used to carry out laboratory work, scientific work, industrial systems and even at the gasoline pump.

A *digital* computer is a computer that represents data usually in digits or bits or discrete signals. It manipulates and performs arithmetic and logical operations on the data. Most computers are digital computers of which there are several classes. We will return to digital computers later in this Chapter.

A *hybrid* computer is a special purpose computer that uses both analog and digital devices to handle continuous as well as discrete signals. With a *hybrid* computer system, the digital and analog subsystems are interconnected so data can be transferred between the analog and digital subsystems via *analog-to-digital converters*; *digital-to-analog converters*. Hybrid computer systems are used in scientific applications, cybernetics and control engineering, and other applications in industrial processing.

The digital computer is the most common type of computer of which six classes are available. The six classes of digital computers are: supercomputers, mainframe computers, minicomputers, workstations, personal computers, and portable computers.

The digital computer accepts *data* in different forms. Data (*singular* **datum**) are any representation, values, numbers, characters or symbols that have been arranged, extracted or performed upon to derive information or for further processing. Therefore, *information* is derived from the arrangement, extraction, analysis or processing of data into a meaningful form. People who work with information as a fundamental part of their jobs are called *information workers*. They include accountants, managers, lawyers, real estate agents, loan officers, consultants, system analysts and data processing professionals, information system professionals and newscasters, and news-reporters.

Besides these *information workers*, there are Government Agencies that gather covert information and news about suspected persons or an enemy. This type of information is called *intelligence*.

Knowledge, Technology and Economic Development

Economic development is a state that is characterized by a change in an economy from agricultural activities to the production of industrial products and a range of services using modern technology. Economists also use the cumulative growth of per capita income, accompanied by structural and organizational changes to identify a state of economic development. However, there is a serious misunderstanding by some economists about economic development. Their economic development models always imply that a country's economy must move or be transformed into a high level of industrialization, which is depicted by the abundance of durable consumer goods and skyscrapers to achieve a state of economic development. This implication is not entirely true. It is a superficial view of development.

A predominantly agricultural economy can generate substantial economic growth. Given the right *knowledge*, a well-educated labor force, the use of technology, enough physical capital, and a "good" infrastructure, agriculture can provide a way to economic growth and improved well-being of its citizens. For it would be ludicrous to refer to the Central Valley of California, or Iowa, or Illinois as less-developed region and states in the United States of America.

Economic growth is often caused by an increase in the supply of factors of production or their productivity. Knowledge, the use of information technology, the adoption of new and improved methods, and innovations are all attributes of economic growth. Economists at economic development agencies need to pay more attention to these attributes and include them in their economic development models.

At the microeconomic level, a firm learns to be more efficient as it gains experience with new products or production techniques. Therefore, it is better to purchase knowledge and technology, and pay foreign firms for their assistance in developing domestic capabilities than to rely solely on the *infant industry* argument and on protection. Also, knowledge, the use of information technology and the adoption of new methods of production will allow a firm to produce goods and services at lower cost than other firms that depend entirely on government subsidy and protection. Besides, the adoption of these factors can lead to improved products, profits, and growth of the firm.

Before moving on to the next point, we must emphasize that the value of knowledge, education, information technology, and training should not be underestimated. To invest in knowledge, education and information technology can be very expensive, but these are necessary conditions for economic and human development.

Human Capital

Some economists have recognized that an investment in knowledge, education and training in a human person gives rise to an increase in productive powers of labor or increased income in the future. This idea was developed into an economic theory called *human capital.*

In economics, capital consists of durable goods capable of producing a stream of goods or services over a period, or a sum of money that is invested in a business enterprise. Capital also includes stocks, stock rights, and bonds, and an accumulation of expenditure that gives rise to subsequent incomes. Thus, capital is a productive resource that yields a return over time. Also, capital derives its worth from the opportunity costs and the returns it yields in the future.

The *human capital investment theory* uses the adjusted "present value method" to evaluate investment in human capital. This theory looks at the knowledge and skills a worker has, as a result of his education and training, including special training that enhances his productivity in the firm where the training takes place. It evaluates the education and training as part of the *stock of productive capital.*

The *human capital investment theory* has been used by Theodore Schultz in *The Economic Value of Education.* It also is used by economists in Labor Economics and political economy to explain certain interesting phenomena in the labor market. This economic theory is based on simple mechanical models using present value methods to evaluate a set of complex subjects involving knowledge, education and economic development. The theory though useful in certain circumstances is very limited. The theory fails to recognize the epistemological nature of the problem, or, the growth and strength of the industrial and commercial competition from other nations, or the *psyche* behind the pursuit of knowledge for its own sake, or the qualitative benefits that knowledge and education bring to a nation.

The Knowledge Industry

The knowledge industry is the production, extraction, processing, storing, transmission and delivery of knowledge. The collective employment of people as a means of livelihood in these areas may be described as being employed in the knowledge industry. Colleges, universities, some corporations, national research laboratories, firms, individuals, publishing, broadcasting, and the government, are all working in or associated with the knowledge industry.

Universities and colleges are in the knowledge business. They generate, transmit and disseminate knowledge through teaching, research, books, learned journals, and from an accumulation of stored knowledge. Instructors and professors are passing on knowledge to the next generation of young people. Also, some of the knowledge disseminated in the many learned journals is new knowledge produced by faculty through research and scholarship. Many of the articles published in these journals are tedious and *prolix minutiae* (narrow with trivia detail) with no interest in laity and outcome. However, some new researches are useful. Moreover, some of these new researches are so important that they have the potential to transform society, or the way we communicate, the way we do business, the way we work, or the way we live.

Colleges and universities can be key institutions for the creation of 21st century society. But organizational innovations and adaptiveness are needed. Their missions must go beyond the missions of the "ivory towers." They must take on added responsibility by learning and teaching people how to use the technology to make the modern civic society more productive and successful. A good university must encourage and try to keep renowned scholars. By doing so, graduate students will want to go to your university to be with the researchers to discover their latest findings, participate with them in research, and learn how to do research, which is an important part of their learning experience.

Corporations, national research laboratories, firms, individuals and government also are in the knowledge business. It is the national policy (at the moment in the United States of America) to support research in universities from federal government funds in the form of grants and contracts. But there is no guarantee that a shift of support will not occur if universities do not adapt to changing circumstances. Some nonuniversity organizations are beginning to receive funding from philanthropic organizations that hitherto was the exception to the norm.

Off-campus educational networks that use computers and information technology, Local Area Network, Wide Area Network including the internet and television networks also are in the knowledge industry. Also, many programs from the Corporation for Public Broadcasting are concerned with the transmission of knowledge.

The collective share of organizations within the knowledge industry is about 40 percent of the gross national product (GNP) of the United States of America, and its growth is more than double that of the GNP. Also, this is a development that may require some rethinking by economists, because such employment activity would have been regarded by classical economic theorists or socialist theorists many years ago as unproductive. But as the world turns, employment activity in the knowledge industry is now regarded as productive, "the new wealth of nations," and capital. The reason for this change is embodied in the nature of knowledge. Knowledge is not static; it is dynamic.

The Value of Knowledge

In economics, value is the intrinsic worth or price of a good or commodity or service. It involves a monetary, or material worth. Earlier economic writers like Aristotle, Adam Smith and Ricardo made the distinction between value in use and value in exchange. But how do we value knowledge in today's economy? Is knowledge a commodity or a property?

Economists have avoided dealing with knowledge because knowledge raises epistemological questions that are more in the domain of the philosopher. However, new knowledge and new fields of discipline have enabled us to inquire beyond the traditional boundaries of economics. First, knowledge itself is hard to classify as a commodity or something that is bought and sold. A possible reason for this could be the difficulty of measuring the quantity of the commodity (*knowledge*) itself. We can put the price on a lecture, a book, or a software, but always find it difficult to put the price on knowledge or have always resisted thinking of knowledge as a commodity. A book, or a software is the product of knowledge and this (product), we can put a price on, based on costs and the supply and demand for that product.

However, knowledge can be property. For example, knowledge about "how to make or produce a product or how to produce a work" is accessible today in the form of either books, computer programs, tapes, television programs, or other published works. From a legal and an economic point of view, a property is the right of possession to which the owner has legal title. As such, it can be exchanged, disposed of or bought or sold. Thus, knowledge is a property. When used in this sense, knowledge can be exclusive or nonexclusive.

In economics and business, the word "exclusive" means not sharing with others, or excluding others, or not including specified items. For example, Company X has exclusive publishing rights. In this sense, knowledge has enormous value, so much so, that the United State Government with other foreign governments signed a treaty to protect a work, which is first published in the U.S. or in another foreign country. This treaty is known as the Universal Copyright Convention (UCC) or the Berne Convention.

From these arguments, we can assert that knowledge is a property. However, this type of property is different from other forms of property, such as a piece of land on which a house stands or that used in farming, or a chattel. It is *intellectual property. Intellectual Property* includes certain creative works, original literature, computer software, trade marks, trade secrets, semiconductor chip masks, and inventions.

Not all knowledge is exclusive. Unlike animals, human beings can communicate through languages, signs and behavior about how we live, how we communicate with others, and how we use tools to better our lives. Modern civilization can pass knowledge to their siblings, children and others through communication, books and published works, training, education and behavior. Because of this historical process, the possession of knowledge and beliefs in one man's head also may be in possession of others. Knowledge can be reproduced and shared by others through communication.

Social and Political Value

The societies of the United States of America, Britain, Western Europe, and Japan, have long accepted that the amenities of an industrialized society depend upon knowledge and cooperation. Also, an increase in industrialization demands an increase in cooperation. Thus, knowledge is a necessary co-producer of better amenities and a productive life. From this reasoning, we can infer that knowledge is better than ignorance, although from time to time some members of our society seem determined to perpetuate a state of ignorance as long as possible.

Knowledge also is desirable for the cultivation of the individual, and to develop the individual's capacities to the utmost. This includes the concern for culture, tradition and pursuing knowledge for its own sake. However, some people opposed to this belief argue that money should not be spent pursuing knowledge for its own sake. The opposing argument ignores the fact there are nonmonetary and qualitative benefits in the pursuit of higher knowledge. These benefits include the joy of knowing, respect in some circles for the educated person, emotion, and the feeling that knowledge is power.

Qualitative Values and Opportunity Costs

Some organizations use education (including college education, and graduate work) and general and specific training, to relate their capabilities and future economic well-being. They make an inventory of skills and capabilities of people within their organizations. This inventory is important not only because management need information about human resources for manpower planning, or for personnel assignment within the organization, but also for assessing quality and capabilities of the human organization.

The knowledge that an individual possesses enhances the value of that individual to the organization. For example, a company may go to a great trouble to attract an executive, manager or software engineer to its organization by paying enormous salary and benefits. The main reason is that an individual may possess certain knowledge that the company wants. Also, in the case of a president or a chief executive officer, upper management may be looking for a person with specific knowledge that may be used to alter or change the organization of that company, or even change the course of development within that organization.

In other organizations, such as colleges, universities, hospitals, and defence contractors, knowledge of their personnel defines the quality and capability of their organizations. For example, a listing of key people with their qualifications, earned and honorary degrees, credentials, and other professional recognitions, can be used to show the capability of an organization to undertake certain tasks successfully to the external world. In many of these organizations, knowledge enhances the human resource socially, psychologically, and economically.

Knowledge brings economic benefits to an organization whose value can be estimated from the subsequent productivity and earnings potential in the future. The value of knowledge also can be measured in terms of *opportunity cost*, the value of a benefit sacrificed in favor of an alternative course of action. At the individual level, for example, if you attend evening classes and summer school, you are sacrificing the enjoyment of free evenings, television, and fun, for the benefits of learning, knowledge, and future job and social opportunities you may receive in the future.

Knowledge also can have extremely high value or can be priceless. This type of knowledge is found in experts or *expert systems*. For example, a patient in a rural or urban area may have to accept less than complete treatment for an infectious disease or possibly die without the knowledge and treatment from an expert in infectious diseases. In this sense, knowledge is *invaluable* or priceless.

The Nature of Knowledge

This topic fits into the domain of the philosopher. It is that branch of philosophy called *epistemology*, which can be traced back to the Greek *episteme* (knowledge, understanding, from *epistanai)*. Knowledge is the possession of a fact or a state of knowing with clarity, such as in knowing that an *integrated circuit* (IC) is a small piece of semiconductor material that contains several interconnected miniaturized electronic circuits. The number of logical components, normally transistors may range from 2 to more than 1,000,000 transistors. Knowledge also is concerned with being aware of a fact or knowing a state of affairs, such as the *yen* has risen by twelve points against the dollar during a certain period.

Knowledge also means the possession of a skill or expertise or abilities in *knowing how* to do, or *how* it works. Knowledge in this sense involves *understanding* or *comprehending* the nature and significance of what is *known*. This type of knowledge is gained through study, or communication with a knowledgeable person or experienced gained through repeated practice, discovery and plausible inference (*heuristics*).

Knowledge has enabled us to make useful tools that change our lives enormously. We understand these tools more than we understand the world around us. The reason for this is that the world around us and the nature of life are more complex than the tools we create.

The television, the computer, the telecommunication and cable networks, the software, and their organizations are simpler than the human being. We also understand these systems and tools better than we understand the human being because we built them to use in an occupation or a pursuit.

It is easier to understand a computer as we will show in this book than to understand the weather or earthquakes with certainty. The reason is that people (including myself) who build computers or develop software want to build a computer system that would work. Therefore, man in order to build something that would work has to build something he understands. From this form of reasoning, we can get a better understanding of knowledge and man's technology and their limitations with respect to knowledge of the human being and our world.

The Seeds of Information Technology and Intelligent Computer Systems

The embryo from which information technology and intelligent computer systems grew may be traced to the earlier stages of three series of works. The **first series** was done by Norbert Wiener and others. This series culminated into a book titled, *Cybernetics: or Control and Communication in the Animal and the Machine* (1948). Wiener with others developed programs for computing machines to solve partial differential equations, mathematical logic to solve switching problems, ideas on time series, information, and communication, feedback, computing machines and models that emulate the nervous system, self-organizing systems, learning and self-reproducing machines and other useful ideas.

Cybernetic concepts have not subsided, but were utilized by other disciplines such as engineering, biological science, robotics, and others. For example, the concept of *feedback* is used by engineers in analyzing and designing practical control systems and other technological devices. Feedback and control systems theory also is used by physical, biological and behavioral science researchers, and students of these disciplines.

Also, some ideas developed in studying switching problems are utilized in the modern Asynchronous Transfer Mode (ATM) system for internetworking. The ATM uses cell-switching and multiplexing technology to handle constant transmission delay at guaranteed capacity and with intermittent traffic, which is associated with packet switching. The ATM is used to bring together Local Area Network (LAN) and Wide Area Network (WAN) subnetwork to perform the switching and routing functions.

The **second series** of work was done by Claude E. Shannon in the *Bell System Technical Journal*, and later by Weaver, who wrote an explanation of the main concepts of Shannon's theory in nonmathematical terms. The works of Shannon and Weaver culminated in a book titled, *The Mathematical Theory of Communication* (1949). Despite advances in technology, many ideas used in modern communication systems are derived in part from the Mathematical Theory of Communication.

Shannon showed that however complex the communication system is, it could be reduced into six essential elements. The block diagram presented below in *Figure 1-1* is a graphic representation of the essential elements of a general communication system proposed by Shannon.

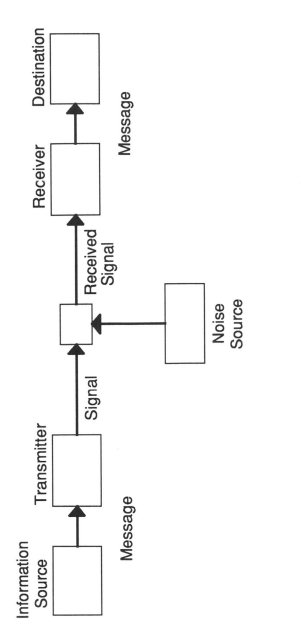

Figure 1-1. Schematic Diagram of a General Communication System

Let us describe these essential elements briefly:

An *Information Source* is the element that produces the message, packet or sequence of messages to be communicated to the receiving terminal or computer. The message may be in the form of text, audio, visual or multifunction combining all three forms.

The *Transmitter* operates on the message or converts it to a signal suitable for transmission over communication channel to a *receiver*. The *transmitter*, which usually is a device, must be capable of converting the message in accordance with the characteristics of the communication channel.

The *Channel* is the communication path or medium used to transmit the signal from the transmitter to the receiver. It ranges from the ordinary telephone line (analog network) to Integrated Services Digital Service Network (ISDN) channels, or a band of radio frequency, television channel, or satellite channel that is provided by an earth satellite system.

Each channel and its capacity is different. For example, suppose that you have a modern PC with a COM port, MODEM, Camcorder and a regular telephone line, and wanted to transmit moving and still images, and audio signals simultaneously to a remote location. How does the capacity affects this communication? Let us take a look at this problem. The MODEM converts the data to analog using sine wave to transmit through the voice network. The typical MODEM for a PC is 14.4 Kilobits per second (Kbps) although a MODEM with speeds 28.8 Kbps are available. However, the bandwidth (the range of frequencies that can safely convey such signals) is not sufficient to provide video, audio, and document transmission simultaneously at an acceptable standard.

To be able to use a camcorder and transmit video, audio and share a document with another person on a computer in a remote location, you will have to use another channel with greater capacity such as ISDN. The ISDN service offers two interfaces. A Basic Rate Interface and Primary Rate Interface. The Basic Rate Interface or BRI contains two 64 Kbps data (D) channel that carries call signaling, setup, and user packet data on the channel.

Also, it is called a 2B+D connection, which can carry a wide range of communication. As a single BRI it can carry two simultaneous voices or data conversations to the same or different locations. The D channel also can be used for packet communications to a third location simultaneously. Moreover, the two B channels can be combined for transmitting data at uncompressed speeds of up to 128 Kbps.

In California, Pacific Bell has made available ISDN to individual users almost to every location at an affordable rate. So we can design an educational network that will enable a student with a MODEM, and a computer with an ST or NTI interface for the ISDN connection. The student also can attach a video camera to his computer, and with the appropriate software be connected to a new type of education and knowledge system. If he is researching on a project or examining a patient and concerned about a diagnosis, he can send a snap shot of the document or symptoms and have a tutor or expert come on line on a one-to-one personal conference and actually see the document or problem that he is working on and get immediate feedback. Also, the student and the tutor or expert would be able to see each other while discussing the problem.

From the example given above, you can see that the capacity of a communication channel was described not only in terms of speeds or the number of bits it can transmit, but rather in terms of the capability of transmitting *information* in its entirety.

Noise

Throughout the course of transmission the signals may be perturbed by *noise*. *Noise* is a disturbance or communications line impairment that affects the signals transmitted. Thus, *noise* can distort the information carried by the signal. There are different kinds of noise, such as ambient noise, burst noise, impulsive noise, and background noise. There is a relationship between *noise* and the accuracy of a message, thus the higher the ratio of noise on a channel, less accuracy is expected of the message. Although you can send the message repeatedly, and statistically you may get different versions thus allowing you to analyze the message and reduce the probability of errors.

Receiver. The *receiver* is normally a device that performs the inverse operation of that done by the transmitter. It converts the received signals and reconstructs the original message signal for further processing in say a computer, terminal equipment or receiving station.

In the example I gave about using ISDN services, the receiving location also must have ISDN services and similar interface, software, and type of equipment. The receiving end of the channel of communication must be capable of receiving or processing the message in its entirety.

Destination. The *destination* is a station, or person for whom the message is intended. Shannon's work is exciting. He takes you into the study of *entropy*, and statistical physics. He also discussed the measurement of information, the mean information content, the average information content of a system and the notion of *entropy*.

Warren Weaver on the other hand looked at communication in a broad sense. He divided the subject into three levels. Level A, technical problem, how accurately can the symbols be transmitted? Level B, the semantic problem, how precisely do the transmitted symbols convey the desired meaning? And Level C, the effectiveness problem, how effectively does the received meaning affect the conduct in a desired way?

The **third series** of works was done by Allen Newell, Herbert Simon and J.C. Shaw. These scholars opened the road to *intelligent* programs. They developed a program called *Logic Theorist* that used *heuristics*, rule-of-thumb reasoning and plausible inference to generate proofs of mathematical theorems. The work on *Human Problem Solving* by Newell and Simon set the pace for the development of expert systems or knowledge-based systems. Although they used the words *information processing program*, their works were close to the works of John McCarthy and Marvin Minsky who were working in the area of *artificial intelligence.*

In *The Handbook of Artificial Intelligence*, Barr and Feigenbaum, defined Artificial Intelligence as "the part of computer science concerned with designing intelligent computer systems, that is, systems that exhibit the characteristics we associate with intelligence in human behavior." AI uses models of intelligent human behavior and try to simulate that behavior on a computer.

Artificial Intelligence often draws on cognitive science theories to develop models of machine learning and Computer-Assisted Instruction (CAI). CAI is based on programmed instructions, but goes beyond the work of Skinner and analyzes a student's performance in order to develop individualized tutoring strategy. This approach brings computers and information technology to the educational process. Also, AI is concerned with robotics, pattern recognition, language, programming, computer science, and expert system or knowledge-based system. The value of this technology is substantial and should not be ignored.

New Opportunities for Sharing Knowledge

Computers and information technology have opened enormous opportunities to obtain and share knowledge world wide through the *internet*. The *internet* is a wide area network connecting thousands (different) of networks in industry, education, government, research and private providers. The *internet* was used primarily for educational and research activities, but now it is open to commercial users and individuals with Personal Computers. New software packages for accessing and navigating the Internet's World Wide Web, and others are coming on to the market to allow PC users to connect to any site in the world. The consequences and effects of the computer and information technology on education, management, science, economics and on sociological development, are enormous. For those people who are still skeptical about computers, put your fear aside, then turn to Chapter 2 and get ready to put this book to work, as this technology is too important to ignore.

Questions for Discussion and Review

1. What is information? As a result of changing technology there is a greater demand for information workers than factory workers in the U.S.A. and Western Europe. Who are information workers?

2. Define the term knowledge industry. Explain the role of universities and colleges in the knowledge industry.

3. If the expected monetary returns are less than the cost of investing in human capital, then why invest in education? Are education and general training good investment? Discuss.

4. Explain how education, knowledge, and changes in technology can lead to improved productivity and a better standard of living?

5. What is knowledge? Explain the difficulty in arriving at the economic value of knowledge.

6. What is cybernetics? Describe a couple of ways in which cybernetic concepts can be of assistance to engineering, education, management, biological sciences, or any other field of discipline.

7. Distinguish between technical communication and communication in the broad sense, including linguistics.

8. Describe briefly the works of two people that opened the road to *intelligent* programs.

Chapter 2 || How Data is Represented Internally in the Computer

Data (*singular* **datum**) is any representation such as characters, numbers, or alphanumeric characters to which meaning is assigned. Data includes variables, constants, arrays, and character strings.

Data is represented internally in the digital computer in binary code. This means that ordinary integer numbers, decimals, fractions, alphanumeric data and character strings must be converted into binary representation for the computer to understand and execute.

Generally, a user will not need to worry about the binary representation of instructions in the computer. However, any intelligent discussion of computer codes and instructions must involve at least the use of elementary mathematical number systems, such as binary, octal, hexadecimal and concepts of bits, bytes and words. Nevertheless, sometimes the question is asked, if users do not need to worry about the binary representation of instructions in the computer, why one should concern oneself with this topic?

Strangely enough, this is a good question. People who use the computer and want to know more about it, or people who write their own programs can learn more about the computer if they know how to communicate with a computer in the instruction that the computer can directly recognize and execute. Also, if we know about bits and bytes, we can understand how the memory is structured.

If we understand computer number systems and the difference between fixed-point representation and floating-point representation, we can understand the type of configuration needed to perform scientific operations as opposed to the configuration required to perform operations on integers or fixed-point arithmetic. Understanding how to convert decimal notation to binary numbers does not mean that we need to do it ourselves. The student or reader will be better equipped to appreciate the development of the computer and its capability when the student has a basic understanding of the internal representation of information in the computer and their number systems.

Charles Babbage, (1792 - 1871), the British mathematician, is the inventor or father of the computer. After finding lots of errors in his mathematical tables, Charles Babbage decided to build a machine that could evaluate polynomial equations more accurately than his mathematical tables could. He called the machine a *difference engine.*

The idea of a *difference engine* was well received and he obtained a grant from the British Government, which later withdrew its financial support. But with help from Ms. Ada Augusta Byron, who later became Countess Lovelace, Babbage continued to work on his ideas. He later built a computer model with cogs and wheels that he called the *analytical engine.*

Babbage's model incorporated five key concepts that form the basis of the modern computer. The five key concepts are:

- Input device
- Processor or number calculator
- Control unit to direct the sequence of the calculations
- Storage to place or hold the numbers waiting to be processed
- Output device

Alan M. Turing (1912 - 1954), John Von Neumann, Norbert Wiener, Howard Aiken, Thomas Watson Sr., John Mauchly, J. Presper Eckert, J. Bardeen, H.W. Brattain and W. Shockley, Seymour Cray, Gene Amdahl and William Norris are among the many industrious people that contributed to the development and use of computers. However, they had one idea in common, and that was, computers could process vast amount of numerical information quickly and accurately.

The numbers that are most familiar to us are based on the decimal notation that uses ten different symbols ranging from 0 through 9. This system uses decimal digits and the radix of 10. However, when you input numbers based on the decimal number system, the computer has to convert these numbers and symbols into the binary number system for the computer to understand. For example, if you try to input the following: $(1 \times 10^3) + (9 \times 10^2) + (9 \times 10^1) + (5 \times 10^0)$, and print the total, or type $\sum \frac{x}{n}$ and supply the data to compute the mean on our computer, it will respond with "Bad command" or it will not obey your instructions using these formats. The reasons are:

First, you have to reduce these algebraic expressions to an expression that the computer understands.

Second, you have to have an interpreter or compiler (a program) that translates and executes each instruction including the expressions into machine language that can be directly executed by the processor of the computer. For example, you may need a BASIC compiler. In BASIC, an expression is a combination of one or more variables, constants, functions, and special characters. Variables are used to express arithmetic calculations, logical comparisons or string manipulation.

Third, if we rewrite the following expression such that

$$(1 \times 10^3) + (9 \times 10^2) + (9 \times 10^1) + (5 \times 10^0)$$

$$1000 \quad + \quad 900 \quad + \quad 90 \quad + \quad 5$$

the computer will represent the numeric data internally in the *binary* number system.

The computer uses the *binary* number system, with a radix of 2 (base 2) to perform its operations. The computer also uses the base 2 number system that contains digits of 0 and 1 to represent numerical values. Thus, when a computation that involves decimal numbers (the traditional number system that human beings use), the computer will execute the following steps:

1. The computer will convert the input data from its decimal format into its binary equivalent.
2. The computer will perform the desired arithmetic operations in binary, and store the result in a register or registers.
3. The computer will convert the binary result into the decimal equivalent, then sends the results to an output device.

The binary number system is used to represent all information in the computer, including programs and data. Each number, character, data item, attribute, or record, is encoded internally as a group of 0s and 1s. Each 0 or 1 is called a binary *digit* or *bit*.

Computer circuits are designed to monitor electrical signals or pulses that are based on a binary two-states ("on" and "off") system. The computer converts information and data into a binary representation where each character, number or object is encoded internally as a group of binary digits or bits of 0 and 1. These digits or bits are based on the binary number system.

Bits and Bytes

A *bit* is an abbreviation of a binary digit, a zero or one, used in the binary number system. It is the smallest unit of information a computer can work with. A group of eight bits is often called a *byte*. It takes one byte of memory to store one character or symbol. A byte is a number of bits in a unit of measurement of computer storage. Very often when a computer project is being designed, we may want to know how many bytes are required to store a program, a page of text, or a relational file. This may require allowance for spaces, control characters and other needed information. We also may want to know how many bytes are free on our hard disk, or on a floppy disk.

It takes many bytes of memory to store a program, a relational data base, or text file on a modern computer system. The unit most frequently used are kilobytes and megabytes. A kilobyte is equivalent to 1024 bytes, 1K bytes (2^{10}) or 1 KB. Examples of byte measurement are, 8K bytes, 16K bytes, 128K bytes... 360KB. A megabyte is equivalent to one million bytes or 1,048,576 bytes (2^{20}) denoted by 1M bytes or 1MB. For example, your computer may have 4MB or 8MB of main memory, and 40MB, 80MB, 420MB, or 540MB of secondary or external memory. A computer system also can have one *gigabyte* of secondary memory, which is equivalent to one billion bytes, 1,073,741,824 bytes or 1GB or 1000 megabytes or 1000 MB.

Bits and Word Size

A group of binary bits may be organized into a predetermined number of bits to be processed as a "word." A "word" is a unit of data that a computer operates upon as an entity. For example, the memory of a computer with an 8-bit microprocessor may be logically structured into 8-bit words. Consequently, a computer that has a 16-bit or a 32-bit microprocessor would have a memory that is structured in 16-bit words or 32-bit words respectively. We also can say that since 8-bits are called a byte, a word size for an 8-bit microprocessor may be regarded as one byte, for a 16-bit microprocessor, 2 bytes, and for a 32-bit microprocessor, 4 bytes and a 64-bit microprocessor, 8 bytes. It follows that a computer with a processor that can process or move, 32-bits or a 4-byte word (chunk) at a clock cycle is a much faster computer than one that can process or move 8-bits, one byte, 16-bits, or 2-byte word. Hence, this is the reason why a 32-bit microprocessor is faster than an 8-bit or 16-bit microprocessor, if the clock speeds are the same.

Binary and Decimal Number System

We have already used the terms "binary digit," "bits," and "0 and 1," but to reinforce our understanding of the binary system, let us examine briefly the binary number system. The binary number system is a positional notation system representing numbers in which the *radix* or base for each digit position is two, "2," and the numbers are represented by the integer digits 0 and 1. We can use the mathematical technique of "place" or positional notation to arrive at a value. For example, in the decimal number system starting from the right most digit displacement of one position to the left means that the digit is multiplied by a factor of 10. With the binary system a displacement of one position to the left means that the digit is multiplied by a factor of "2."

In many parts of the world, the number system that people use in their daily lives is the *decimal* number system. It is made up of ten parts, and all the numbers that people work with, are based on the radix of "10" (ten) with the symbols: 0, 1, 2, 3, 4, 5, 6, 7, 8, 9. With the decimal number system, we use a combination of symbols to represent a value greater than 9. For example, to represent "twenty," we put 2 to the left in the "tens" place and zero in the "ones" place. Similarly, to represent the number 1995, you can put one 1 in the "thousands" place, 9 in the "hundreds" place, 9 in the "tens" place and 5 in the "ones" place. The decimal number 1995 also means 1 times one thousand (1 x 1000) plus 9 times one hundred (9 x 100) plus 9 times ten (9 x 10) plus 5 times one (5 x 1). Thus, to express 1995, we write:

```
      1 x 1000 = 1000
      9 x  100 =  900
      9 x   10 =   90
  +   5 x    1 =    5
  ──────────────────────
                  1995
```

We can express numbers in an algebraic manner using the progression of power from right to left such that one thousand (1000) is written as 10^3 (10 x 10 x 10), one "hundred" is written as 10^2 (10 x 10) and "ten" is written as 10^1. We can use the same system for numbers express in the base 2 number system. Let us use the decimal number system and the binary number system to express: 100110. At a glance, it could be expressed as "one hundred thousand one hundred and ten." However, if this number is a base 2 number, then it is the decimal equivalent of thirty-eight (38) or 100110_2 in binary. *Figures 2-1 and 2-2*, show the position values of 100110 in the dcimal and the binary number systems respectively.

10^5	10^4	10^3	10^2	10^1	10^0
100000	10000	1000	100	10	1
1	0	0	1	1	0

```
100110
```
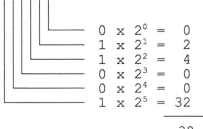

```
0 x 10⁰ =        0
1 x 10¹ =       10
1 x 10² =      100
0 x 10³ =        0
0 x 10⁴ =        0
1 x 10⁵ =  100000
          _____
            100110
```

Figure 2-1. Decimal Place or Position Values

2^5	2^4	2^3	2^2	2^1	2^0
32	16	8	4	2	1
1	0	0	1	1	0

```
100110
```

```
0 x 2⁰ =   0
1 x 2¹ =   2
1 x 2² =   4
0 x 2³ =   0
0 x 2⁴ =   0
1 x 2⁵ =  32
         ____
           38
```

Figure 2-2. Binary Place or Position Values

The computer is often used to store and process very large numbers. This numbers must be converted into the binary number system. For example, 100101100 base 2 is the equivalent to 300 in base 10. Thus, base 10 is more convenient for humans to represent numbers than is base 2, which is the basis of the binary number system. Binary numbers can be grouped to form binary codes that represent alphabetic characters, numbers or special symbols such as 7-bit ASCII code. Binary numbers also can be easily grouped to represent other numbers that are a power of 2, like 8 and 16. These units are more convenient for humans to work with when analyzing data and/or problems.

Different Sets of Numbers

The computer also can handle different sets of numbers, such as *integer, real,* and *floating-point* numbers. *Integer* numbers are those numbers that make up a set of positive and negative whole numbers or zero. They have no decimal points and no fractional parts. Examples of integers are:

0	2	4	8	16	32
0	+1	+3	+5	7	64
1	−2	−4	−6	−15	−32

Real numbers are numbers that contain a decimal point, such as 0.5, 1.0, 2000.125, 8.75, -7.25, 12345678.09

Real numbers may be represented in two ways. The first is, by *fixed point representation* and the second is by *floating-point representation. Fixed point representation* is a method of number representation in which the decimal or binary point is fixed in a given location and the number contains a constant predetermined number of digits. In the case of fractional numbers the position of the *radix point* (i.e., the decimal point in the decimal system) is located at a fixed predetermined position.

If you are writing a program and want the computer to carry out arithmetic in fixed point, then you must communicate this fact, as well as the position of the base point to the computer. The incoming numbers will be stored in a fixed-point storage unit called fixed-point words. If the binary point is defined to be to the left of the second bit in a word, the binary number 110110 would be interpreted as 1101.10 and all the operations would be based on the definition, thus,

```
1101.10
1110.10
1001.10
1001.01
xxxx.xx
```

In business, many calculations are carried out in dollars and cents. So if you are doing calculations in dollars and cents, then you can define each word so two digits to the right of the base point are maintained.

The second way of representing real numbers is by *floating-point representation*. In this representation, a number is represented by two sets of digits, known as the *fixed point part* and the *exponent* or characteristic. If a number n is represented by a fixed point part a and an exponent b, then $n = ar^b$, where r is the *radix* or base of the number system either 10 for the decimal system, or 2 for the *binary* system. For example, using base 10, a floating point representation of the number 0.0002345 is:

0.0002345
becomes
0.2345 (*mantissa*)
x 10^{-3} (*where -3 is the exponent*)

This type of number representation is more conducive to scientific computation than normal business transactions of dollars and cents.

Floating-point representation helps computers perform calculations more accurately. Some computers have a processing unit feature that provides floating point registers to perform floating-point arithmetic calculations. In some Personal Computers, there is a microprocessor support chip that supplements the operations of the central processing unit, to enable them to perform complex mathematical and floating point calculations in parallel with other operations. This micro-processor support chip is known as a *numeric coprocessor,* and is often called a *math coprocessor.*

A *chip* is an integrated circuit (IC). And, a *microprocessor* is a processor whose elements are miniaturized into one or many integrated circuits. It is a functional unit that receives, interprets and executes instructions in a computer.

Floating-point operations are measured in *flops* per second. For example, one MFLOPS means one million basic floating-point operations per second.

Base 8: The Octal Number System

Another number system used in computers is the *octal number system.* The octal system uses the digits 0, 1, 2, 3, 4, 5, 6 and 7 and the radix is eight. The lowest integral weight is 1. And octal number may be evaluated using either the remainder method or the expansion method. Let us use an example to illustrate the remainder method to determine the octal equivalent of 347 in the decimal number system. Remember that we are using base 8, thus:

Remainder Method:

$$
\begin{array}{r|r}
8 & 347 \\
\hline
8 & 43 \quad\quad 3 \\
\hline
8 & 5 \quad\quad\; 3 \\
\hline
8 & 0 \quad\quad\; 5
\end{array}
$$

Using the remainder in reverse order, $347 = 533_8$

Base 8 is a convenient way for representing base 2 numbers because 8 is a power of 2^3, hence $2^3 = 8$. Base 8 also is used as a shorthand way of representing a string of binary bits. For it is easy to convert octal to binary. So, in the above example, to convert 533_8

(octal) to binary, we simply replace each octal digit from right to left, with the three binary digits that represent 533_8. Thus,

```
  5          3          3      base 8
 / \        / \        / \
101        011        011      base 2
```

Many computer manufacturers produce computers that use binary and octal. Also, many terminals use 7 bits plus a parity bit to represent input data in the computer. This code scheme is an octal base scheme.

The American Standard Code for Information Interchange (ASCII), pronounced "askee" is the code scheme used by most terminal devices. ASCII Code was developed in the 1920s when data was transmitted by codes through teletype machines. Today, ASCII code is used in microcomputers and for data communication. A character is coded using 0s and 1s in various combination of bits, so each character would have its own coding of bits, thus its own bit configuration.

Now, let us use the following table, *Table 2-1* to show the equivalent decimal numbers, 0 through 16, using base 2 (binary) and base 8 (octal).

Table 2-1. Decimal, Binary and Octal Equivalent Values

Base 10 (decimal)	Base 2 (binary)	Base 8 (octal)
0	0000	0
1	0001	1
2	0010	2
3	0011	3
4	0100	4
5	0101	5
6	0110	6
7	0111	7
8	1000	10
9	1001	11
10	1010	12
11	1011	13
12	1100	14
13	1101	15
14	1110	16
15	1111	17
16	10000	20

Base 16: The Hexadecimal Number Systems

Another type of number system, which is used in the computer is the *hexadecimal* number system, sometimes called *hex*, it uses the radix (base) of 16.

The hexadecimal number system is quite different from decimal in that it uses the 16 digits: 0, 1, 2, 3, 4, 5, 6, 7, 8, 9, and characters A, B, C, D, E and F, where the characters A, B, C, D, E, and F correspond to the decimal numbers 10, 11, 12, 13, 14, and 15 respectively. The radix is 16 in which the lowest integer is 1.

When counting in hexadecimal, we do not carry over to the next place until we reach the first numbers past F. The following table, *Table 2-2* shows the equivalent decimal numbers, 0 through 15 using base 2 (binary) and base 16 (hexadecimal).

Table 2-2. Decimal, Binary and Hexadecimal Equivalent Values

Base 10 (decimal)	Base 2 (binary)	Base 16 (hexadecimal)
0	0000	0
1	0001	1
2	0010	2
3	0011	3
4	0100	4
5	0101	5
6	0110	6
7	0111	7
8	1000	8
9	1001	9
10	1010	A
11	1011	B
12	1100	C
13	1101	D
14	1110	E
15	1111	F

An advantage of hexadecimal number system is that eight binary digits can be encoded as two hexadecimal symbols. Generally, humans would prefer to handle a two-symbol code rather than an 8-bit binary number. Also, when a program is being tested or an attempt is being made to diagnose a software error, a memory dump can be made to output the contents of the location or status at the time of its failure in *hexadecimal*. Programmers find the hexadecimal code lines easier to read than binary code lines of zeros and ones.

Codes

A code is the representation of data or instructions in symbolic form, sometimes used as a synonym for instruction. The instruction code is a code that represents the machine instructions of a computer. It cannot be modified by a user. The machine instructions (generally expressed in binary) for a computer can be executed directly by the processor of that computer. Thus, the machine instructions in one computer can be different from another computer produced by different manufacturer. So, to compensate for this difference, one of the following code schemes may be adopted: EBCDIC or ASCII.

EBCDIC (Extended Binary Coded Decimal Interchange Code) pronounced "eb-see-dick" is one of the most popular internal codes for the digital computer. EBCDIC was developed by IBM and used extensively in the IBM 360/370 models. In this code system, eight bits are used for coding a character, or a byte.

EBCDIC coding also is divided into two parts. The first part consists of a 4-bit code called the *zone*, and the second part consists of a 4-bit code, which is the digit portion, and sometimes called a *nibble*. With EBCDIC, characters are represented as 8-bit structures with the capability of generating 256 characters.

The second commonly used code for representing numbers, letters and special characters is ASCII code. In an earlier section of this Chapter, we described the characteristics of ASCII code, but it was not until 1963 that it became a standard code suitable for information transmission. This octal code system contains seven bits for information and one parity bit. A *parity bit* is a check bit appended to an array of binary digits to make the sum of all the binary digits, including the check bit, always even or always odd. Normally, a parity check is performed automatically by the hardware.

Sometimes in *asynchronous communication,* we may have to set the parity option to get the connection established. The parity option might be even, odd or none. When an 8-bit code scheme is used, the parity option is likely to be none, whereas, it will generally be even or odd with a 7-bit code scheme.

The United States government adopted the ASCII code as a standard, and today it is used in a variety of microcomputers all over the world. ASCII code is commonly used as a transmission code for both telegraph and data communication in U.S.A.

Machine Language

Machine language refers to *instructions* written in *machine code*, which can be immediately obeyed by a computer without translation. It also is synonymous with computer language.

Human beings do not like to deal in numbers and digits only, they prefer to deal with letters, words and *symbolic instructions*. In the early development of the digital computer, computer programs were written in *machine language*, which was recognized and executed by the computer's Central Processing Unit (CPU).

Machine language instructions are composed of an *operation code* and an *operand*. The operation code, or *opcode* represents the operation the computer must perform. This may involve an action being performed on one or more data items, such as adding, multiplying, comparing or moving.

The *operand* is the item on which an operation is performed, or that which is operated upon. An *operation* is a well-defined action that, when applied to any permissible combination of known items produces a new item. For example, adding 5000 and 3000 and obtaining 8000.

The numbers 5000 and 3000 are the operands. The number 8000 is the result. The ADD is the operation code indicating that the operation performed is addition. In hardware concepts, three registers will be used. Two *registers* will store the two data items or operands. A *register* is an addressable memory location in a computer. And the third register will be used to store the operation to be performed. In this example, the second register also is used to store the result of the operation thus replacing the second operand. When this is done, it is called the *accumulator register*, as it accumulates the result of successive operations.

Assembler Language

To solve a problem by writing in machine language can be time consuming, difficult, tedious and costly. A language called *assembler* is developed for each kind of computer produced to reduce the cost and time of writing in machine language. *Assembler language* permits the use of English and symbols to designate the processing operations and data names. Assembler language is a source language that includes symbolic machine language statements in which there is a one-to-one correspondence with the instruction format and data formats of the computer. But to use this language, you must have an *assembler*, a translator or computer program that converts assembly language instructions into object code.

Further, whether you are using *assembler language* or a *high-level language* like Pascal, BASIC, COBOL (Common Business Oriented Language), C++, the programs will still be processed in machine language. For all programs executed by the computer are actually processed in machine language, because it is the language that the computer uses when executing a program. By now we should understand how information is represented internally in the computer, and how the different internal codes are used when we enter data into a computer.

The computer is an excellent tool in helping to solve problems. But first, we must define the problem, and decompose the problems into its constituent parts, then specify a set of well-defined rules or procedures for the solution in a finite number of steps. This approach is called an algorithmic approach from the term *algorithm*. The development of an *algorithm* may involve flowcharting and decision logic. We will explore these methods in the next Chapter.

Questions for Discussion and Review

1.   Distinguish between integer number, real numbers and floating-point numbers, giving examples of each.

2. What is mega flop?

3. Why are the concepts of the binary number system important to an understanding of the digital computer?

4. Which of the following are valid binary number?

    (a) 1001   (b) 1300   (c) 10011100
    (d) 9626   (e) 1100.011   (f) 01A

5. Convert the following values as stated:

    (a) 98 (decimal) to binary
    (b) 0101111 (binary) to decimal
    (c) 10^4 to binary
    (d) 0101 (binary) to octal
    (e) 1996 (base 10) to hexadecimal

6. What is the difference between a bit, a byte and a word? Giving examples of each?

7. What is fixed-point representation?

8. Describe a processing feature of the modern computer that performs floating-point calculations.

9. Explain the term machine language.

10. What are the advantages and disadvantages of assembler language?

Chapter 3 | Algorithm and Programming

T he need for specifying the logical requirements of a problem goes beyond theoretical mathematics and computer programming. Even Government Departments need to develop some kind of orderly sequence of instructions to help employees and citizens solve problems using the various rules and regulations. For example, in a modern society, rules and regulations proliferate. After a while these rules and regulations impinge on more people who may not have the time, inclination or ability to study them.

The authors of these regulations argue that the ordinary citizen can easily understand the regulations. But unfortunately, an understanding of the English language and a knowledge of grammar are not sufficient to avoid ambiguity and difficulties in following Government rules and regulations. The reason is words alone cannot convey the meaning of certain regulations accurately. Another reason is that words have a kind of fascination to some people. Words make some people want to use or misuse them to build a mystique around ordinary activities.

A way to make rules and regulations intelligible is to develop an algorithm. With an algorithm, people can follow a sequence of instructions of "rules and procedures," or "general guidance" to receive proper advice or be assured of a successful outcome. With the technology and tools that are available today, you may need to use a computer system to help develop the right procedure for solving the problem.

Two of the more important computing procedures that lead to a solution of a problem are *algorithms* and *heuristics*. However, in this Chapter, we will discuss *algorithms* and defer our discussion on *heuristics* for the latter part of this book.

Algorithm

An *algorithm* is an ordered set or list of well-defined mathematical and logical procedures that can be followed to solve a problem in a finite number of steps. An algorithm can be expressed in any form and language. But not every list of instructions constitutes an algorithm. Therefore, an algorithm must satisfy at least three criteria.

1. The steps, operations, or instructions must be finite, and of a reasonable length so that they can be processed and a final result can be offered.
2. Each instruction must cause one or more actions to take place by a computer or the operations named to be performed must be executed by some external action. For example, an instruction could be a calculation to be performed, a condition to be tested, or an instruction to change or alter the flow of control.

    A program is made up of a sequence of instructions each of which directs the computer to perform a specified activity. The total collection of instructions provides the computer with a step-by-step procedure to accomplish a specific task or solve a problem. The processing of a program may include the use of an assembler or a compiler to prepare the program for execution. The computer can then process the compiled machine language instructions.
3. The algorithm must enable the execution of the program to end at some point.

Program

In today's marketplace thousands of programs (*software*) are available to meet a variety of needs and applications. So, some people ask "Why do we need to know about programming when we can go out and buy a program (*software*) and use it to solve a problem?" It is not surprising to hear this question. This is a consumer's view of computers. However, experience has shown that people who have a knowledge of programming are better able to understand the programs (*software*) and the computer systems as opposed to people who have no knowledge of programming. Besides, if for some reason you cannot find an existing program to solve your problem for you, or you cannot find a person to write a program for you, then if you have a knowledge of programming, you can possibly write a program for yourself. Therefore, knowledge of programming is valuable. The skills you acquire in learning to program will sharpen your approach to problem solving. Besides, you can learn to program a computer for the fun of it and develop programs that play games, or create music. After all, these are important activities that aids in one's intellectual development.

Steps in Program Development

Before you rush to the terminal or your PC to compile a program, there are five steps you should follow in developing a useful program. They are as follows:

The first step is to define the problem. This is a critical step that should involve the user of the program, the programmer, and the systems analyst. Cooperation is important in order to ensure that the program solves the actual problem at hand.

The second step is to analyze the problem. This includes developing the solution path, mapping out the logic of the program and the computer operations necessary to solve the problem.

The third step is to prepare a flowchart or *pseudocode*, which is a set of instructions that are logically structured but does not follow the syntax of any particular programming language.

The fourth step is to code the program, which means translating the logic of the flowchart or pseudocode into a computer program. Thus, to write the instructions in a high-level programming language according to the logic outlined in the flowchart or pseudocode.

The fifth step is to run, execute and debug the program. This step includes detecting, locating, and eliminating errors in your program.

Developing an Algorithm and a Computer Program

Computer professionals have developed many tools for developing algorithms and programs after a problem has been defined. Two of the more important tools are *structured design*, and *flowcharting*.

Structured design requires you to decompose a problem into a hierarchical structure of parts called *modules*, which can be separately compiled. The design is a *top-down* design where each program is designed by first developing the overall picture or fundamental purpose of the program. Then, the purpose is broken into subcategories that describe each aspect or function of the program. Each of these subcategories corresponds to a specific program module that can be coded independently.

Each module should be small and simple within the limits dictated by the efficient use of programming and the operating system. Structured design has a control module at the top level of the hierarchy with detailed modules that descend into the lower levels of the hierarchy. This means some modules may be nested (a module within another) and each nested module or *subroutine* will have only a single entry and a single exit point.

With structured programming a *library* of modules or sub-routines may be created and used in other programs as needed. Also, the location of problems and errors in a program may be more easily traced to a particular module when the program is designed using the structured methodology. Furthermore, structured design allows effective use of modules and subroutines that have already been tested by manufacturers and users. A tested module or sub-routine can be easily incorporated into a new program thus giving the programmer an advantage in writing complex programs.

As a general rule, before you write a program or draw a flowchart you should dissect the problem into parts and arrange these parts to form a solution to the problem. Also, you should make a plan with some tentative steps or procedures to follow that will lead you to solve the problem.

The first step is to *analyze* the problem. This involves under-standing the problem. To accomplish this, you should:

- Write down a statement in plain language, about the nature of the problem to be solved.
- Determine the type of data you will provide to the computer for execution.
- Determine the output that will constitute a solution to the problem.
- Determine the computation and logical processes the computer must perform to convert the data provided into a solution (output).

This approach can help you develop an algorithm or a set of instructions which, when followed will produce the solution to the problem.

Flowchart

The preparation of a flowchart is an intermediate step between developing the algorithm and writing the program. The flowchart is a graphical representation of the process or steps required to solve a problem, using suitable symbols or annoted geometric figures connected by flow lines for the purpose of representing an algorithm or designing a program.

Program flowcharts use specific symbols to represent different activities or actions. The following symbols are the most commonly used symbols, and have been adopted by the American National Standards Institute and other International Standard Associations. See *Table 3-1* next page.

Table 3-1. Flowchart Symbols

SYMBOL	NAME	MEANING
	Start/End	Each Program has a beginning and an end.
	Input/Output	Indicates when an input, read, or output operation is to be performed.
	Process	Indicates an operation such as a calculation, or data manipulation.
	Flowline	Represents the flow sequence.
	Decision	Represents a decision point or question that requires a choice of which logical path to follow or a condition to be tested.
	Connection	Connects parts of the flowchart.
	Preparation	Indicates a preparation step, as in describing a FOR/NEXT loop or DO loop.
	Predefined Process	Indicates a predefined process where the details are not shown in this flowchart as in calling subroutine.
	Annotation Flag	This is used to add clarity or comments.

	Document	This symbol is used in system flowcharts to indicate a document such as invoices, transcripts, references, test scores.
	On-line	This symbol represents a file that is in storage on-line.
	Magnetic Tape	This symbol represents a removable tape with files.

Flowcharts are the most frequently used method for developing algorithms and writing programs. They are independent of computer languages. A flowchart, if drawn with diligence and care, can be converted easily into a program using any programming language.

In contrast with the detail steps required for drawing a flowchart for an algorithm or a computer program, there are other types of flowcharts. For example, there are *systems flowchart* and *block diagrams*.

A *system flowchart* is an important tool used by a system analyst. A system analyst is a person who investigates a real or planned system to determine the information requirements, and methods, procedures and processes of the system, and how these relate to each other and to any other system. It is a diagram of the operation of a system that shows the relationship between files and programs. An example of a system flowchart is given in *Figure 3-1*.

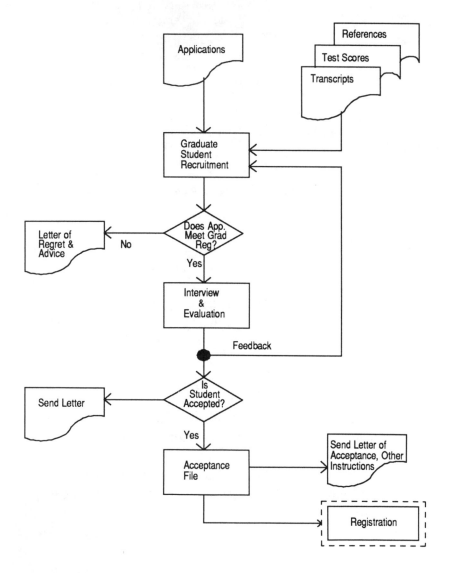

Figure 3-1. System Flowchart for a Graduate Admissions' System

Another type of flowchart is called a *block diagram*. A block diagram is a diagram of a system in which the principal parts or functions are represented in blocks connected by lines that show their relationships. See *Figure 3-2* below showing a block diagram for a control system with feedback elements.

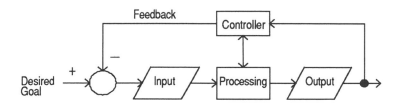

Figure 3-2. Block Diagram of a Control System with Feedback Elements

In the remainder of this Chapter, we will use flowcharts to develop specific algorithms and describe the logical structure and processing sequence of a computer program. So, let us move to the problem below and develop a program to solve the problem using a computer.

Write a program to calculate the gross wages of an hourly temporary worker, Olga Perez. Calculate the gross wages, output the gross wages, and then stop the computing process.

Plan of Problem:

Object:	Program to calculate gross pay
Assign:	Temporary worker's name, Olga Perez
Assign:	Hourly rate: $12.00
Assign:	Number of hours worked: 40
Computation and logical process:	Multiply hourly rate times hours worked
Output:	Gross pay header and the amount of the gross pay

The flowchart to perform these steps is shown below:

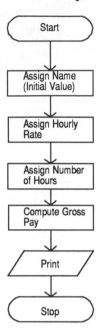

Figure 3-3. Program Flow Chart

Writing (*Coding*) the Program

Writing instructions for a computer is sometimes called *coding the problem*. This involves translating the problem-solving logic from the flowchart into a computer program or instructions. But first, you must choose a computer language in which to write your instructions.

In this Chapter, we have chosen to use BASIC (Beginner's All-purpose Symbolic Instruction Code), a high-level language. A high-level language is a programming language whose concepts and structures are convenient for human reasoning. For example, BASIC, PASCAL, Ada, FORTRAN and COBOL are high-level languages. High-level languages are independent of the structure of the computer and its operating system.

With high-level languages each statement corresponds to several machine language instructions. Also, you have to have a specific compiler or interpreter in order to use the particular language. A *compiler* is a program that translates instructions written in a high-level programming language such as BASIC into machine language.

The reasons for choosing BASIC are: that BASIC is used in many practical applications, particularly in small organizations. BASIC is the simplest computer language that is widely available on most low-cost microcomputers. The time required to learn BASIC is the shortest of all programming languages. Also, the enhancements to BASIC have made BASIC a powerful language.

Elements of BASIC Programming

The purpose of this section is not to turn you into a programmer. But, it is intended for you to learn what programming is like, and after a taste of it, you may find you want to learn more. It also fulfills part of our procedure in developing algorithms and writing a computer program.

How to Write Simple BASIC Programs

In BASIC, each instruction is composed of three parts: the *line number, the statement* and *the variable or variables*. The *line number* identifies the instruction and makes it easy to refer to. The *statement* is an instruction, which directs the computer to perform a specific task or declare certain information that the computer needs. A *variable* is a name used to represent a data item whose value can be changed while the program is running. The *variable* is not the data itself, rather it identifies a location in memory where a particular data item is stored. Variables store either numeric or string values. Thus, *Figure 3-4* shows the three parts of a BASIC program.

Figure 3-4. A Diagram of Three Parts of a BASIC program

The compiler or interpreter reserves certain words that direct the computer to perform a set of actions or to declare certain information the computer needs. Let us look at some of these reserved words or BASIC *statements* below:

The REM Statement

REM statements are used as a comment statement so you can document your program properly. In addition, REM statements are used in programs to identify or describe a program, to add a line as spacing for ease of reading, to define the variable names used in the program, and to describe segments of a complicated program.

You do not need to use quotes, " ", in the comments or remarks, otherwise, the computer will display the quotation sign as well as the text within the quotes. The format for a REM statement is:

line number REM any remarks or text on the line

For example:

10 REM PROGRAM TO CALCULATE GROSS PAY ***

Some programmers like to use stars or dashes to highlight their REM statements.

The LET Statement

The **LET** statement is very useful statement in BASIC, and is sometimes called the *assignment statement* or the *replacement statement*. With assignment statement, the data-item name usually is first, and the value to be assigned to the data-item name is stated after the equal sign.

For example:

ASSIGN Hourly rate = 12.00
ASSIGN Number of hours worked = 40

The word **LET** is often used to mean "assign" in primitive statements, thus:

```
LET R = 12.00
LET N = 40
```

The format for the LET statement is:

Expression

line number LET variable name = Variable

Constant

The LET statement also evaluates or places the value indicated in the expression on the right-hand side (of the "=" symbol) in the storage location (variable) indicated by the variable on the left-hand side of the equal sign. The statement:

10 LET T = **420** (means store 420 in location T.)

The Let statement can be used with *strings* in the form of alphanumeric symbols. Alphanumeric symbols include alphabetic characters, numbers, and other commonly used symbols. The following statement illustrates the assignment statement with a *string*.

20 LET G$ = "GRADUATE STUDENTS"

You can use either single or double quotation marks before and after the string, GRADUATE STUDENTS. In this example, the double quotation marks contain seventeen characters (including the blank character). The LET statement tells the computer to replace the contents of G$ by the string expression to the right of the equal sign. Note that the variable location that stores the alphanumeric characters is identified by a $ sign so the computer can distinguish between numbers and words.

The LET statement also is used to instruct the computer to perform computations, such as

50 LET T = U * C + 90
60 LET T = T + 50

Look at statement 60, Algebraically, this statement makes no sense. However, in programming languages this statement says take the value in the location T, add to it 50, and place this new results in location T.

As you can see, BASIC uses certain operation symbols to perform the computation desired. The five main symbols used to perform arithmetic operations are:

+   Addition
-   Subtraction
*   Multiplication
/   Division
**   Exponentation (raising to the powers) or ↑ or ∧

Standard mathematical functions such as SQR(X), LOG(X) INT(X), AND COS(X) and others also are available.

These standard functions are called intrinsic functions because they are a part of the BASIC. They are stored programs or subprograms (subroutines) which are built into the language, and to make use of them, it is necessary to call them into a particular program and provide a value for them to operate on.

For example:

20 LET S = SQR(64)
    or
20 LET S = SQR(X)
    or
30 LET T = INT(G+1)

The PRINT Statement

The PRINT statement is an output statement. It causes the computer to display the value of the contents of a memory location, string and/or expression and the result of a program in a mode that humans can understand. The PRINT statement also is used to control the horizontal spacing of variables, constants, strings, characters, and vertical spacing of data lines. The format for the PRINT statement is:

line number PRINT list (of items you want to print)

The following statements are valid examples of the PRINT statements:

```
60   PRINT "GROSS PAY = $ " ; P
90   PRINT 15 * U ——— Expression
100  PRINT B ———— Variable
110  PRINT R , S ——— List of two variables, R and S,
                        the output of R and S.
```

You will notice that quotation marks are used with the PRINT Statement in line 60. This causes the characters (string) including the blank spaces that are inside the quotation marks to print exactly as they appear when the program is executed.

The *semicolon* (;) is used as a delimiter in the PRINT statement. It causes the computer to print the next variable in the next print position on the same print line after the string.

The use of *commas* (,). When you use commas to separate items in a PRINT statement, the data to be displayed are automatically divided into *print zones* or fields that are normally 14 spaces wide. Usually, there are five *print zones* or fields per line. In a 72-character line, the last two character positions are not used. Examples of using commas with the PRINT statement are:

```
40   PRINT "SEPT", "OCT", "NOV", "DEC"
60   PRINT "FAHRENHEIT","CELSIUS"
```

Let us use the flowchart on *Figure 3-3* and code the program by typing the following on your terminal or computer after loading your BASIC compiler.

```
10  REM PROGRAM TO COMPUTE GROSS PAY ***
20  LET R = 12.00
30  LET N = 40
40  LET P = R * N
50  PRINT  " OLGA PEREZ " , " GROSS PAY = $ " ; P
99  END

RUN
OLGA PEREZ      GROSS PAY = $480
```

INPUT Statement

The INPUT statement allows data entry to a program from an external source, either from a user on an interactive basis or from the programmer or a device while the program is running. When an INPUT statement is involved, the program execution is interrupted and the program will display a question mark (?) on the terminal or screen.

The computer waits for the user to interact by entering a value or values and pressing the Enter or Return key to inform the program to continue executing. Usually, the *prompt* or question mark is preceded by information from a PRINT statement, which may include some questions such as "ENTER FOUR TEST SCORES" and "DO YOU WANT TO CONTINUE." This informs the user that he or she has to input data and press the Enter key to continue the program.

Besides the reasons mentioned above, the use of the INPUT statement is of practical importance in dynamic situations where the values of the variables are likely to change each time the program is executed. For example, in weather forecasting, the temperature, winds and clouds change frequently. The format for the INPUT statement is:

line number   INPUT list of variables

Where the list of variables contains variable names separated by a comma in the exact sequence of the data items entered. You will have to enter the corresponding value for each variable in the list of the INPUT statement.

For example:

```
30  PRINT "ENTER FAHRENHEIT DEGREES"
40  INPUT F
     .
     .
     .
30  PRINT "TYPE NUMBER OF CREDITS, COST PER
        CREDIT"
40  INPUT N,C
     .
     .
```

.

30 PRINT "AMOUNT OF PRINCIPAL"
40 PRINT "CURRENT RATE OF INTEREST"
50 INPUT P
60 INPUT R

.

.

.

Let us write a simple program using the INPUT statement to input temperatures in Fahrenheit and print those temperatures in Celsius. Perhaps at a later date, you can improve this program by including winds levels, and movements. But for now, we start with the temperature. The formula for converting Fahrenheit to Celsius is:

$$C = (F - 32) \times 5/9$$

Plan of Problem:

Object:	Program to convert a temperature from degrees of Fahrenheit to its equivalent in Celsius
Print:	Prompting message to remind user of what data are to be entered
Input:	Values of F from terminal
Computation and logical processes:	Compute conversion of temperature of degrees Fahrenheit to its equivalent degrees in Celsius
Output:	Display columns for Fahrenheit and Celsius and the temperature value of degrees in Fahrenheit and Celsius

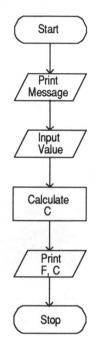

Figure 3-5. Program Flowchart - Fahrenheit Conversion

The program to convert Fahrenheit to Celsius is as follows:

```
10  REM PROGRAM TO CONVERT FAHRENHEIT TO CELSIUS
20  PRINT "ENTER FAHRENHEIT DEGREES"
30  INPUT F
40  LET C = (F - 32) * 5 / 9
50  PRINT
60  PRINT "FAHRENHEIT", "CELSIUS"
70  PRINT F,C
99  END
RUN
ENTER FAHRENHEIT DEGREES
? 68
FAHRENHEIT    CELSIUS
   68            20
```

The READ and DATA Statement

The READ statement is a data entry statement. For when you instruct the computer to READ, it logically expects you to provide the computer with a DATA statement, which stores in the program values to be used in a program by a READ statement. Therefore, if a READ statement is used in your program, then there must be at least one DATA statement in your program.

The READ and DATA statement provides another way to enter data into a program. When you use a READ statement, the computer searches through the program until it finds the first DATA statement. The computer then assigns the data values consecutively to the variable names identified in the READ statement. The DATA values must match the READ list specification both in mode and in sequence.

The format for READ and DATA statement is as follows:

line number READ variable list
(place commas between each variable).

line number DATA list of data items

Where each data item is either a string constant, or numeric constant, with a comma separating each data item.

For examples:

```
50  READ E$, S, Q
60  DATA "SCHOOL OF EDUCATION", 8000,900000
    •
    •
    •
    •
30  READ U
40  LET T = 15 * U + 90
80  DATA 490
```

The IF/THEN Statement

The IF/THEN statement is a conditional branching, or transfer statement. It requires the computer to test if a certain condition is *true* in the program and then, based on one of two possible results, take proper transfer of control action. There are several forms of the IF statement. In this Chapter, only the simple IF/THEN statement is discussed. The general format for the simple IF/THEN statement is:

line number IF condition THEN line number

line number IF condition GO TO line number

If the condition tested is true, control is transferred to the statement number that follows the word THEN or the words GO TO. If the condition tested is *false*, the next statement following the IF/THEN statement is executed.

For example:

   120 IF A > 89 THEN 150
             or
   120 IF A > 89 GO TO 150

Either statement may be used with the same results.

The relational operators that can be used in conditional statements in BASIC are:

=	equal to
< >	not equal to
<	less than
< =	less than or equal to
= =	approximately equal
>	greater than
> =	greater than or equal to

Note. Some computer systems use the # sign instead of < > for not equal. Also, do not use a space between the two signs in the not equal, less than, the greater than, or the approximately equal operators.

In BASIC, there also is a GOTO statement, which is an unconditional branch or transfer to the statement specified by the line number. GOTO statements cause the program to transfer control to another executable instruction specified by the line number. This is mandatory and no condition has to be satisfied as in the IF/THEN statement. The format for the GOTO statement is:

line number [GO TO] line number
[GOTO]

The GOTO statement is frequently used in combination with conditional transfer statement, IF.

END Statement

The END statement terminates the program. And, since the END statement is the last statement in your program, you must assign it the highest line number of the program. The format for the END statement is:

line number END

For example:

399 END

Run, Execute and Debug the Program

RUN is a system command and is not a statement in the program. So after you type *RUN* without any line number, the computer begins to execute the program you have written. In the case of MS-DOS QBASIC, RUN is on a menu, which you may select. Also, you can use the *LIST* command, which will cause the computer to list the program lines.

As the program is entered, you will be notified of syntax problems associated with each statement as it is entered into the computer. Certain errors can be determined only at execution or compilation time. When errors are detected, the computer will halt, you must correct the errors, then you can try to run the program again.

Saving your Program

In order to retain your program for future use or revisions, you must give the program a specific name. It must not be longer than eight characters. After the *END* statement, type *SAVE*, and the computer will place a copy of the contents of the program in the user's working memory onto a permanent storage with its assigned name. Save is an item, which you choose from a menu in MS-DOS QBASIC. If you make changes to an existing program, remember to type *REPLACE*, otherwise, the changes you made will not be stored on your disk. To retrieve a program, type *OLD* followed by the name of the file.

Questions for Discussion and Review

1. "Any citizen with a knowledge of the English language and grammar can understand Government rules and regulations easily, why use flowchart, logic trees and algorithms." Discuss.

2. What does the term *algorithm* means? Describe a couple of techniques you would use to find a solution to a problem.

3. Describe the steps that must be taken in developing a computer program from the initial idea to solving the problem.

4. In what way is learning a high-level programming language useful? Give three reasons for using BASIC as a programming language.

5. Distinguish between a system flowchart and a block diagram. Give examples.

6. What are the advantages of structured design? What are program modules?

7. What is the usefulness of developing a plan of the logical structure and drawing a program flowchart of a problem? Is it not better just to get on the terminal or computer and write the program and not waste time with developing plan and drawing a program flowchart? Discuss.

8. Write a program to compute an invoice amount, using the INPUT statement. The output of the invoice should be in columns as follows:

   Units Sold, Price Per Unit, Total Value
   The initial data items are: Units sold 150, Price per unit is $24.95

9. Write a program to read customer name, customer credit limit, and customer account balance. The data given are as follows:

   Customer Name: Juan Gonzales
   Credit Limit: $4,000.00
   Current Balance: $2,102.50

10. Modify the program in Figure 3-5 to print the message "Caution Heat Causes Dehydration", if the temperature is greater than 106 degrees Fahrenheit.

Chapter 4 ‖ The Computer Revolution

The word *revolution* often connotes a sudden political overthrow brought about by some militant vanguard of a nation. The *computer revolution* was not like that; rather it was a series of technological developments that occurred over a period of fifteen years. It brought a recognizable momentous change in computing and data processing. The change was so extensive that it permeates throughout industry, banking, education, commerce, medicine, national defence, entertainment and other aspects of social life.

The computer revolution started in the United States of America, more specifically in California. California was a State where lots of research activities were taking place. It was a place where many Defence contractors were producing high-tech systems for the military and space research. Also, there was *Silicon Valley*, an area located about sixty miles south of San Francisco and renowned for the manufacture of integrated circuits. The neighboring communities of Palo Alto, Mountain View, Sunnyvale, Santa Clara, and Cupertino were all involved in either Research and Development activities or the manufacturing activities of electronic goods and equipment in one form or another. Moreover, the economic environment was ripe, as it encouraged *laissez-faire*, and the State Government did not interfere with commerce nor did it impose then high corporation tax for doing business in California. It was the belief that free enterprise would foster technological innovation and economic growth.

The exact time when the *computer revolution* started is debatable. Also, it is argued by some people that the *computer revolution* is not yet finished, and it is still taking place. Nevertheless, we can identify four main developments occurring at different periods that caused and effected a recognizable change that is collectively called *the computer revolution.* They are: (1) *the development of the microprocessor,* (2) *interactive computing,* (3) *rapid technological developments in the personal computer market, and* (4) *user-friendly systems that consider the computer a tool for personal productivity instead of a machine for computing.* Let us take a brief look at each of these developments below.

(1) The Development of the Microprocessor

The development of the microprocessor was the most significant advance in electronics since the development of transistors by William Shockley, John Bardeen and Walter Brattain at Bell Laboratories around 1948. The use of transistors in computers led to a reduction in the size of computers equipped with *vacuum tubes.* However, the microprocessor had drastically reduced the size of computers even further, as well as increased the processing performance of the functions of the modern computer. A single *IC* or *chip* contains *Large Scale Integration* (LSI) and *Very Large Scale Integration* (VLSI), a technology that integrates thousands or millions of transistors on a single Integrated Circuit (IC). As a result, a single *IC* or *Chip* the size of a thumbnail or a key on your keyboard can implement the functions of the CPU, thus providing a processor on a chip. *Figure 4-1* gives a sketch of a processor.

Cyrix CX486-DX2 Microprocessor

Figure 4-1. A Sketch of a Microprocessor

To augment the development of the microprocessor, *Integrated Electronics Corporation* (Intel), Zilog, Motorola, and others were able to improve their technology for achieving high density of LSI and VLSI, which can be seen in the recent generation of microprocessors that are currently on the market. Also, semiconductor companies were able to automate their manufacturing processes for producing microprocessors and other integrated circuits, so as to step up production and lower the unit cost of each *chip* produced. The two main factors that influenced the development of the microprocessor were the growth of the microcomputer industry and competition from other semiconductor manufacturers at home and abroad.

We will look at some recent developments of the microprocessor in the section on the development of the personal computer. But now let us turn to another development that has contributed to this change.

(2) Interactive Computing

The second important development in the computer revolution was the availability of *interactive computing*. This was made possible by the introduction of the hard disk, which provided for direct access processing.

The drive behind *direct access processing* came from the Commercial Airlines and Banks. They wanted update information on seats available (American Airlines SABRE System) and banks wanted to know the up-to-date balance on a customer's account.

Besides these corporate clients, students, researchers and scholars saw a need for *interactive computing*. Users wanted to be *on-line* and communicate with the computer through a terminal in the form of a dialogue or conversational mode, back and forth. This environment was extremely productive for users who got immediate feedback, and for programmers who needed to run, test and debug their programs successfully without having to wait hours or days for a response from the computer. This was in contrast to batch processing and off-line processing, which was the only method available to students, researchers, and programmers that were not employed on systems with direct-access processing.

Timesharing provided an alternative to batch processing and off-line processing. It allowed users to pay for the services of *interactive computing* on a time-used basis plus an overhead charge. With time-sharing, several users through individual terminals can share the use ("time") of a computer on what appears to be simultaneously. The tremendous speed of the CPU and rapid transfer rates of the disk storage device made it possible for many users to interact with the computer as though each user alone was interacting with the computer. In short, timesharing allows several users to execute programs concurrently and to interact with the program during execution.

Remember that before timesharing, students, researchers, and users had to learn programming, and supplied their instructions to the computer on a *coding form* to a computer center. As it was not very long ago, probably within your own life time, the following scenario was the norm.

Students and programmers had to carefully fill their FORTRAN and COBOL Coding Forms and follow certain steps in order to compile a program. For example, in COBOL, columns 1, 2, 3 are for page number, column 7 is reserve, and columns 8 to 72 are for program statements. Besides this format the student or programmer had to write in block capitals on the coding sheet. The statements had to be grouped in four divisions:

> IDENTIFICATION DIVISION
> ENVIRONMENT DIVISION
> DATA DIVISION
> PROCEDURE DIVISION

These divisions must all be present in a complete COBOL program.

After coding the program on the coding form, punched cards had to be prepared on a *keypunch* device. To read these cards into the computer, the deck of cards had to be placed face down in the hopper of a punched card reader. The *punched card reader* picked out the bottom card and moved it by rollers to a read station where the punched holes were translated into electrical pulses and sent to the computer's memory. When all the cards were read, they were moved to a *stacker*.

Students and programmers who worked in the above environment will recall that the average *turnaround time* — the elapsed time between submission of a job and return of the completed output — was two days. Also, if the full stop (or period) after the ENVIRONMENT DIVISION was too small or was left out, the student had to debug the program; put in the period, and after making sure that the period was clear enough, resubmit the job to computer room. When the job was completed and the student or programmer got the correct answer the second time (making the total time four days), the student was elated. Looking back, not so long ago, this was a costly and time-consuming process. There was no immediate *feedback,* and corrective action could not take place quickly enough, thus lowering the student's learning curve or level of learning. This state of affairs caused students to lose interest in computers.

(3) Rapid Technological Developments in the Personal Computer Market

The development of the personal computer can be traced back to 1974, where Ed Roberts, the President of MITS, a company in Albuquerque, New Mexico sold hobbyists' kits to people wanting to build their own microcomputer at home. However, companies like Tandy Corporation, Texas Instruments and Zenith Heath built and sold kits to hobbyists. Radio Shack, a division of Tandy Corporation sold the TRS-80. Commodore Business Machines entered the personal computer market with a personal computer called PET (Personal Electronic Transactor), which was successful in Europe and in the United Sates. Other companies like Atari, Hewlett-Packard, and Texas Instruments also produced computers.

In 1976, Steve Jobs and Steve Wozniak, founder members of the Apple Corporation at Cupertino, California produced a series of personal computers for hobbyists using an 8-bit microprocessor, and replaced the complicated switches-and-lights in the front panel with a keyboard. The Apple Computer Company was formed in 1977 and produced many personal computers in its first five years, but two of the most popular models were the Apple II and the Apple II Plus.

The Apple II was sold with Integer BASIC (Beginners All-purpose Symbolic Instruction Code), a high level programming language imbedded on Read Only Memory (ROM) chips. The immediate response that appeared on the screen when you switched on the computer was a " > " prompt. The prompt indicated that the Apple II was ready for instructions in Integer BASIC.

The Apple II Plus had an autostart ROM that would switch on an external disk drive (if attached to the computer) and load the operating system. The operating system was on a diskette, which was inserted into a disk drive or to disk drive 1 (if there was more than one disk drive). The Apple II Plus also had Applesoft BASIC in ROM and used this symbol "]" as the prompt. The operating systems were called DOS for Disk Operating System. There was DOS 3.2 and DOS 3.3 in use at that time.

The Personal Computer was a great success. It brought the computer to the people. It was used by students, parents, children and anyone who wanted to buy one. The explosion of interest led to a rush to develop and write application software for these computers. Component manufacturers rushed to produced "add-on" or enhanced components for these computers. However, some large computer manufacturers felt that since some of the programs used on these personal computers were just games and small word processing programs, personal computers presented no threat to them because their programs were not adequate for business and professional purposes. But to students this was a coveted opportunity to have an interactive system at their disposal when compared to having to use punch cards or waiting to get a chance to sit at a terminal that was heavily requested. Personal computers were later found to be useful tools for improving programming skills and for gaining an under-standing of mathematics.

There were other companies including some large electronic companies from Japan that entered the personal computer market.

They used Zilog's Z80 processors and CP/M (Control program for Microprocessor) as an operating system for use with their computers. A large number of these computers were also shipped with BASIC. CP/M is a product of Digital Research Corporation. The CP/M was stored on diskettes and had some good features. It encouraged application programs in education, entertainment, and programs to solve commercial and scientific problems. It also encouraged the development of personal programs.

The IBM PC. In August 1981, International Business Machines (IBM) Corporation introduced a personal computer known as the IBM Personal Computer (PC). The IBM PC was based on the 8088 microprocessor. The 8088 was derived from the 8086 microprocessor and was modified to accommodate an 8-bit external data bus and other inexpensive 8-bit peripherals. IBM took advantage of available "off the shelf" components, but introduced an architecture that was bold, open, and unfolding. New knowledge, schematics, and information on science and technology was freely disseminated, thus breeding an inventiveness and a willingness to produce software and "add-on" devices for the IBM PC. There also was a willingness to accept change.

The IBM PC Architecture. The architecture of a computer is the overall design and layout of the main hardware components, their principal features and how they are interconnected as a computer system. The IBM PC architecture was open and freely discussed. The hardware components of the IBM PC consisted of: an Intel 8088 microprocessor, which ran at a clock speed of 4.77 MHz. It had a 16K RAM on the system board and used 4116 chips with a maximum of 200 ns, 160K diskette drives with monochrome text only monitor, and a cassette port. The architecture included the CPU, timing circuitry, memory input/output subsystem, and bus conductors. The system board had a Direct Memory Access (DMA) controller with four DMA channels and five Input/Output (I/O) Expansion slots. It had a Read Only Memory (ROM), Basic Input Output System

(BIOS), which facilitated the transfer of data and control instructions of the computer's hardware and peripheral devices such as disk drives, display unit (monitor), keyboard and so forth. The BIOS was requested by interrupt calls.

PC-DOS/MS-DOS. The operating system was called PC-DOS, which was produced by Bill Gates of Microsoft Corporation, then a small company. PC-DOS was a single user operating system. PC-DOS was marketed by IBM, and a slightly different version was sold as MS-DOS (Microsoft Disk Operating System) by Microsoft Corporation. PC-DOS allowed popular business programs written for the CP/M operating system to be easily converted for use on PC-DOS computers. It also had some new features that made it simpler to use.

IBM XT. The IBM PC received immediate acceptance as the original version was enhanced with 64K RAM on the system board. But in 1983, IBM introduced an IBM XT (eXtended Technology) version of the PC with a 5 MB hard disk drive, 320K diskette Drive, 64K standard memory upgradable to 256K RAM on the system board and a color-graphics' adapter.

IBM exhibited its PC architecture "openly." IBM published schematics, technical details and invited third party manufacturers to develop and market their own enhanced boards and software for the PC. The IBM PC/XT and other options became very popular and escalated into one of the fastest growing markets. Because of the success of the IBM PC, new vendors sprang up everywhere. Companies such COMPAQ Computer Corporation, AST Corporation, KAYPRO Corporation, Osborne Computers, and even larger companies, such as AT&T, Texas Instruments, Olivetti, Zenith, Xerox Corporation and others all rushed to produce personal computers based on, or similar to, the IBM PC architecture. They used MS-DOS which was similar or almost indistinguishable from PC DOS. The result was that IBM had captured (gained the greater share of) the PC market. The other computer manufacturers that were making "IBM PC compatible" or "clones" also had a significant share of the PC market. There were a variety of IBM compatibles or clones. The term compatible meant a functional similarity of hardware device that can use peripherals and run popular software intended for the IBM PC. There were all kinds of claims about compatibility. Some PC compatible manufacturers claimed that their PCs were 100% compatible with IBM software and accessories devices while others were less compatible than some.

In response to the IBM PC and PC-compatible market, application programs for word processing such a WordStar, dBase (database management); spreadsheets like Multiplan and Lotus 1-2-3, accounting packages, and a host of business software started to emerge. Also, customers were beginning to push IBM to expand the memory of the IBM PC/XT.

IBM Personal Computer AT. In 1984, IBM introduced a set of personal computers based on Intel's 80286 microprocessor. This was the AT (Advanced Technology) Computer. The IBM AT-computer brought significant improvement to the PC and PC XT. It had a 16-bit data bus and was capable of addressing up to 16MB of RAM. It also had higher capacity floppy disk drives, battery CMOS memory for storing information on configuration of the computer, 16-bit as well as 8-bit expansion slots. The 8-bit I/O bus of the PC was extended to 16-bit and was designed to accommodate some 8-bit as well as 16-bit adapters (AT expansion boards). The system board had a socket for an 80287 numeric (math) coprocessor, which is a chip that performs mathematical computations including floating point calculations at speeds up to 100 times faster than the microprocessor alone. The IBM/AT design allowed many applications software that was written for the PC and PC/XT to be used on the IBM PC/AT computer.

The standard base memory was 512K or 640K. Also there were other features such as an Enhanced Graphics Adapter (EGA) that supports 640 X 350 pixel resolution displays with 16 colors from a palette of 64 and an expanded BIOS.

PC-DOS and MS-DOS were updated to 3.1, 3.2 and 3.3 with some new features that resemble a part of UNIX. Some of the features include APPEND, BACKUP/RESTORE, FASTOPEN, FDISK, INPUT/OUTPUT REDIRECTION, JOIN, MODE which included COM3, COM4 to its communication package, and some other useful features.

The IBM PC/AT was very successful, and resulted in more computer manufacturers and third-party vendors entering the PC market. There also were new kinds of PC/XT and PC/AT "compatibles" or "clones" which were called either "generic" or simply "clones." They had no trade marks and were shipped partly assembled for a computer dealer to assemble in the correct configuration, and were made in either Taiwan, Hong Kong, Korea or Singapore. They were relatively easy to assemble and cost far less than the earlier IBM PCs. There also were several enhancements, some of which enabled PC/AT clones to achieve clock speeds up to 16 MHz.

Real Mode and Protected Mode. The Intel 80286 was a more advanced microprocessor than the 8088 microprocessor. Among other things, it has the capability to operate in either "real" mode or "protected" mode. Real mode is where a program is allocated a specific location in memory and is allowed direct access to peripheral devices on a single-user computer system. This mode works well, but when more than one program is loaded into memory simultaneously there is nothing to stop one program from unintentionally entering the other loaded program's memory location or try to access a peripheral device simultaneously. When either of these situations occur the system will experience an unstable state or "crash," thus requiring you to reboot the computer system to recover from the crash. Hence, there is no hardware memory protection in such circumstances.

The Intel 80286 microprocessor has the capability of providing "protected" mode so when programs are running simultaneously, each program is allocated its own memory space. If one of these loaded programs then tries to address memory outside its allocation that process will terminate the program, thus protecting other programs form entering that program's memory space. Programs running under protected mode cannot access peripheral devices directly as in real mode. Protected mode provided an opportunity for some simple "multitasking" operations.

The IBM AT and AT-compatibles presented professionals with a powerful single user computer that could be used on the top of a desk with sufficient processing capability to handle professional programs and place control for the processing in the hands of the end user. This notion spread so fast that large corporations, such as banks, insurance companies, finance companies, accounting firms and many more were using microcomputers to do their tasks in preference to minicomputers or mainframe computers where an external resource such as a central database was not needed.

Industrial Standard Architecture (ISA). The popularity of the IBM AT and Compatibles have led to an Industry Standard Architecture (ISA). The ISA was adopted by a group of vendors who had made commitments to, and investment in, devices for the AT. They wanted to lay down some standards to meet the industry needs. The bus architecture was one of the main points of focus, as this type of bus soon acquired the name, "ISA bus."

(4) User-Friendly Systems that Consider the Computer as a Tool for Personal Productivity

The term *user-friendly* is an expression describing a program, system or device that can be easily used by a person with little or no experience with computer or data processing training. To capture a share of the personal-computer market, some software developers and hardware manufacturers realized that they had to develop inexpensive software that nonprogrammers can use with little effort. Also, they had to provide tutorial programs and telephone support to make their software easy to use. Thus, people did not have to learn programming to use the computer or run a program.

Hardware manufacturers caught on to the idea of *user-friendly* and produced personal computers that were easy to connect and supported by installation or diagnostic programs that lead you through an installation with a series of questions, to which you type in answers. Vendors that ignored the idea of *user-friendly* eventually lost market share.

However, the IBM-PC and IBM-PC Compatible computers continued to dominate the PC-Market. They used various versions of PC/MS-DOS Operating System from Microsoft Corporation. These computers use the command-line syntax as the interface. So after you connect your PC and start DOS, this is what you see.

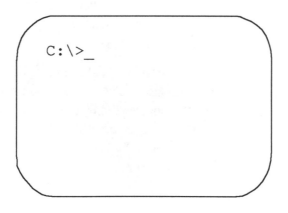

Figure 4-2. The Command Prompt on Current Drive C

The blinking underline that follows ">" symbol is the *cursor*. It shows where the next character will appear when you type or press a key. It also tells you that DOS is waiting for you to type a command. But what command?

You have to know what command and how to write the syntax. Let us look at the syntax for entering a command.

Most modern personal computers use a fixed (hard) disk, and DOS assumes drive C is the primary drive. In the example in *Figure 4-2*, DOS is indicating that C is the current drive but you can start DOS from a floppy disk in drive A in which case it would be as in *Figure 4-3*.

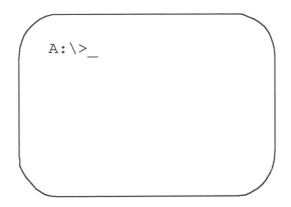

```
A:\>_
```

Figure 4-3. The Command Prompt on Current Drive A

Let us get back to *Figure 4-2* and the command line syntax. The format is as follows:

Command Drive-letter:\Path\Filename Target/P or S

Where *command* is the name of the instruction you want to give the computer. *Drive letter* indicates the drive where the directory or files that you are working on are stored. The back slash (\ ) refers to the root directory, and the *path* is the route of the subdirectory names the computer must follow to arrive at the file you wish to access. You need to specify the path with a filename only if the file is not in the current directory. The *filename* is the name of the file, which may consist of no more than eight characters, which must be followed by a period (.) and an *extension* of three characters, if any. *Target* or *destination* is not applicable to all DOS commands, but it is used when copying a file. The *target* is the file or device to which you want to send the object being copied. This can be either a drive letter and colon, a directory name, a filename or a combination.

P, denotes *parameters*. *Parameters* qualify the action of the command that you want MS DOS to act on. And, *s*, denotes a *switch*. A *switch* is a forward slash (/) followed by a letter (/p or /w) or a number to modify the way a command performs a task.

Suppose you want to copy the subdirectory C:\temp to another disk and rename it asignmts. The command is:

C:\>xcopy c:\temp a:\asignmts / s / e

Suppose you want to display the directory of the disk in the current drive one screen listing at a time. The command is:

dir/p

You can deduce from the above examples that there are certain rules governing the construction of a well formed command, and that a user must know either how PC/MS-DOS works or at least, what information is needed to use PC/MS-DOS to get his work done. Thus, to use a software package you had to learn the rules, a number of commands, and remember them.

If you did not use the software regularly, you could easily forget the rules and commands, and without some *cue* or *clue* this could become an obstacle towards the use of computers. Some software companies like Ashton-Tate, Lotus Development Corporation, Microsoft Corporation, WordPerfect Corporation and others produced tutorials on how to use their software. Also, WordPerfect Corporation went further and dispatched trained representatives to visit dealers and train their staff how to use WordPerfect. This was a resounding success. But still there were many people who wanted to use the computer, but found the commands difficult to remember and the computer intimidating.

While the PC market was growing there was a great deal of advanced research taking place on interactive computing and graphic displays at Xerox's Palo Alto Research Center (PARC), Stanford Research Institute, MIT and other places. However, Steve Jobs, the co-founder of Apple Computer Corporation was interested in the graphic technology and in fostering close relations with PARC.

In 1983, Apple computer Corporation introduced an impressive computer, called *Lisa*. It had sharp graphics and used icons, mouse, and menus. It was too advanced for the mass market then, and cost up to $10,000. But late that year, Apple unveiled to journalists a new portable computer called the *Macintosh*. This made big news as the main television network carried the story.

In January 1984, Apple Computer Corporation unveiled the *Macintosh*, which later became known as the *Mac*, see *Figure 4-4*. The Macintosh brought a revolution to microcomputer users. It introduced a graphical user interface instead of the command-line interface. It also used a mouse to position a pointer on the screen and *click* the mouse button to select from a menu or to perform a function.

The Macintosh computer was accepted eagerly by novice users. The developers of the Macintosh computer wanted their computer to be exciting and easy to use. They also tried to insulate the users from the technical details associated with computing. To accomplish their goals, they included two unique features to their computer architecture. The first feature was an environment based on the metaphor of *desktop* that uses real-world graphic images like documents, folders, and wastebasket, and a see-and-point user interface. And the second feature was a *toolbox* of common routines, functions and a common standard that software developers can build on.

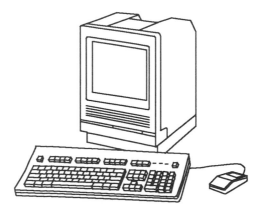

Figure 4-4. Apple's Macintosh Computer

The Macintosh was a success, and since its inception in 1984, the Apple Corporation has enhanced its toolbox, added larger printing capability, digital sound synthesis, and other features. However, it was not very long before other companies like Microsoft and IBM introduced their graphical user interface.

In 1987, Microsoft Corporation introduced Microsoft Windows as an extension of the DOS Operating System. Also, in the same year, IBM and Microsoft Corporation introduced Operating System/2 (OS/2). They both used menus and graphical user interface (GUI).

In 1990 Microsoft released MS-DOS Version 5.0 which included not only its command-line interface, but the MS-DOS Shell, a new graphical interface with pull-down menus.

With MS-DOS5, if you are at the command prompt, you can start the DOS Shell by entering the command **dosshell** and press the Enter key ⏎ . This command will start up the DOS Shell. The DOS Shell had the following.

- The *title bar* at the top of the screen
- The *menu bar,* which shows the names of five menus: *File, Options, View, Tree* and *Help.*
- Below the menu bar is an *area* for drive icons
- Also, there is an *area* for *Directory Tree*, which appears on the left, *a file listing*, which appears on the right.
- A *Main area* displays the *program listing* and an *Active Task List* to display programs that have been started after you enable the *Task Swapper*. With the *Task Swapper* enabled, you can run more than one program at the same time and swap between them.
- *Selection cursor* that shows which item has been selected.
- *Scroll bars* that move part of a list into view.

Meanwhile, in November of 1989 through the spring of 1990, Microsoft and Zenith Data System cosponsored a research project to identify the differences in the performance of graphical and character-based user interfaces for applications software. The research was conducted by Temple, Barker & Sloane, Inc.

The research findings revealed among other things that in a white-collar (office) environment GUI users *work faster* and *work better* (completed more tasks) than CUI users in the same period. Also, experienced GUI users accomplished 58 percent more correct work than experienced CUI users during the same period. The report concluded that GUI generates higher output per work-hour, higher output per employee and lower levels of frustration and fatigue, and greater return on information technology investment than CUI. Also, users were able to master more capabilities of their system and require less training and support.

The transition from computers and peripheral devices that occupy large rooms with special controlled environment and people with special "clean" overcoats to the less expensive and more productive desktop computer or workstations can be described as a *revolution*. Fifteen years ago, the people who used computers were programmers, researchers, engineers, mathematicians, students and system analysts. Today, most of the people who use computers do not have backgrounds in these fields, nor in programming. In fact, most people that use computers today use them to get their work done more quickly and efficiently. The computer is used as a productive tool to help them do their jobs better.

Also, the PC is rapidly becoming a tool for communications and group productivity. The PC is increasingly being used to communicate, access, retrieve, and manipulate information from any part of the world through the *internet.*

The Internet

The *Internet* was developed out of a need to connect individual networks, or for *internetworking* a set of networks into a larger entity. The Internet can be called a *meta-network*, or a network of networks.

The Internet originated from a research and development project that recognized the need for scientists and researchers to connect heterogeneous computer networks that were dispersed at geographically distant locations to share knowledge and information efficiently. This project was sponsored by the U.S. Advanced Research Project Agency (ARPA). ARPA invited universities to participate in the project. Also, other companies like Honeywell and the RAND Corporation provided their expertise in network design, packet-switching nodes, or Interface Message Processors (IMPs). The project later became known as the ARPAnet.

ARPAnet got considerable acclaim after Dr. Robert Kahn demonstrated at an international conference on computers in 1972, how he can connect a terminal to many sites. Internetworking became desirable and this effort led to the development of TCP/IP (Transmission Control Protocol/Internet Protocol), a suite of communication protocols that support peer-to-peer connectivity function for both local and wide area networks. These developments culminated into the internet.

The internet was used primarily for educational and research activities. These activities include exchanging messages, and sharing timely data and information. It also was used for sending data to supercomputer and mainframe facilities across the country.

The internet gave faculty and students of colleges and universities, which had substantial resources, access to resources of other universities, public library catalogs, and databases. Besides, it provided the means for researchers at different universities and laboratories to share data and do collaborative work on computational intensive problems such as atomic spectrum, meteorology, environmental analysis, and earthquake prediction.

Today, the U.S. Government is interested in building a nation-wide network infrastructure that will provide the next generation of networking facilities, which Senator and Vice President Albert Gore, called the "Information Super Highway." The internet is now open to people and businesses that are outside the scientific and academic communities. This development has led to some radical changes.

People with PCs were able to get user accounts, thereby gaining access to the internet through independent Internet Access Providers. End-users used the internet primarily for exchange messages, such as electronic mail (E-mail) and for other on-line services.

The changes also provided the opportunity for a company like Netscape Communications Corporation to develop user-friendly software with graphical user interface and "hypertext" to enable novice users to navigate, "browse," and explore the World Wide Web (WWW) without having to learn UNIX. As a result of these developments, a person using say, the Netscape navigating program, can with the click of a mouse, look at documents in London, France, Germany, Stockholm or Tokyo. Other Internet tools and services like, Usenet (Network News), WAIS (Wide Area Information Servers), FTP (file transfer protocol), which allows for efficient transfer of files between systems and Gopher, are becoming easier to use. So, more people are logging on to internet sites.

The internet is changing rapidly, and a global interconnected computer community is rapidly approaching. There is a computer revolution, and no educator, nor educational administrator should ignore it.

Questions for Discussion and Review

1. Give three examples of how computers have revolutionized the way of performing an operation in your establishment, or the ways of doing business.

2. Explain the meaning of IC, LSI, and VLSI.

3. What are the desirable characteristics of the micro processor?

4. Explain the following terms:

    Interactive computing
    Timesharing

Turnaround time

Off-line processing

5. Distinguish between command-line interface and graphical user interface.

6. Explain why they are more people who are not programmers or data processing experts using computers today?

7. MS-DOS5 allowed you to work with DOS two ways. Describe two ways you can work with DOS5.

8. What is an analog computer, and explain its uses? What is a hybrid computer, and why is it used?

9. Explain what is meant by the following:

Industrial standard Architecture

An IBM Compatible computer or a "clone".

10. The Intel 80286 was a more advanced microprocessor than the 8088 microprocessor. It had the capability to operate in either "real" mode or "protected" mode. Explain what is real mode and protected mode.

Chapter 5 | The Anatomy of a Computer System

In Chapter 1, we said they are six classes of digital computers. We can easily describe the structure of any class of digital computer and its parts. However, since we want the reader to become familiar with computers, we decided to use a modern PC because it is readily available to the reader. With the modern PC, the reader can examine, analyze and study the computer system in real terms.

System Fundamentals

A system is an arrangement, set or collection of things connected or related to form an entity or a whole. A simple way or shorthand for representing a system is through a block diagram. A simple form of block diagram, *Figure 5-1* is a three-block pictorial representation of the cause and effect relationships between the input and the output of a physical system.

Figure 5-1. A simple Block Diagram of a System

This diagram has a universal application for many forms of systems. The *input* for example may be regarded by some as the stimulus or excitation applied from an external energy source in order to produce a particular response.

The rectangular box (in the middle) is the factor that acts upon or does the processing or operations to be performed on the input to yield the output. In computer terms, this could be the central processing unit.

The *output* is the actual response obtained from the processing unit. Thus, it is the yield or the transform in a transformation process.

The arrow → represents the direction of unilateral information or signal flow. You can develop a mathematical relationship of this concept of a system by representing it by way of a differential equation such that:

x is the input

$\dfrac{d}{dt}$ is the operation

and, the output y is $y = \dfrac{dx}{dt}$

This method of a representing system is called an *abstract system*.

We can use the same diagram as in *Figure 5-1* to describe the organization of computer hardware. Thus, a computer hardware may consist of an input unit (keyboard), a system unit (processing unit) and an output unit (monitor) connected to form an entity. Notice that I use the word *hardware*.

The term *hardware* is used to define the physical components and peripheral devices of the computer equipment. However, the *hardware* is only part of the whole of an information system or a knowledge system.

A Cybernetic Model of a Man-Computer System

The study of general system theory and cybernetics helps a person to build a suitable model to solve a system problem. The model helps one to visualize or conceive of the system or to analyze, evaluate or study it further. Therefore, let us extend the three-block diagram to include *software* and a *person*, who could be a user at the office.

To study the computer as a system, let us use a cybernetic model to explain the relationships of the elements of the system. This cybernetic model includes the theory of control systems based on communication (the transfer of information) between the system and its environment, and the control of the system's function in regard to its environment.

In *Figure 5-2*, we include a person in the system. The person has two *inputs*. First, he is able to observe the output of his perception and take cognizance of the response coming out of the system. And second, he is able to have inputs directly from the environment. Also, there is a reinforcement control system, which is a correlating program. On the basis of the goal(s) and from inputs the system receives, the correlating program decides whether the performance of the user is correct or incorrect. On this principle, the system can be designed to reinforce some responses, or give clues, or ask the user questions. Hence, the foundation for an *intelligent system.* We will return to the topic of designing an intelligent system later in this book, but for now, let us describe the components or *elements* of a real computer system.

The Computer as a System

A computer system consists of: (1) *hardware*, which is the physical machinery of the computer and a set of peripheral devices that are associated with that computer, and (2) *software*, which are programs and instructions that tell the computer what to do. In essence, a computer system consists of the hardware and software in interaction, as an "organized whole." A Simple Block Diagram of a Cybernetic Model of a computer system with feedback is shown in *Figure 5-2*

Feedback is an attribute of a closed-loop system that permits some of the output or a controlled variable of the system to be compared with the input to the system so the appropriate control action may be formed as some function of the output. The *feedback* linkage (-b) from the goal, which is a comparator, represents negative feedback. Feedback also can be positive in which case it will be + b in the linkage.

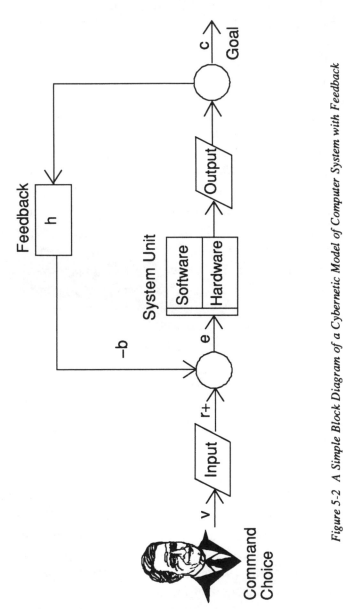

Figure 5-2 A Simple Block Diagram of a Cybernetic Model of Computer System with Feedback

In control engineering involving hydraulic systems and power steering systems, we can have both positive and negative feedbacks in the design of a control system for, say, an aircraft or luxury automobile power steering system. The notion of *feedback* is used in electrical, chemical, mechanical, and economic systems as well as the central nervous system. Now, let us turn to the other *elements* of the computer system.

Software - Types of Software

On its own, a computer is just a collection of equipment or hardware and peripherals. A computer cannot do anything useful for the ordinary person without programs, called *software.* There are four major types of software: *system programs, compilers or language processors, development tools,* and *application programs.*

System Programs. System programs include the operating system, which is a layer of software that lies between the computer hardware and the *application programs.* The operating system controls the operation of the computer system and handles the details of managing the hardware resources, accessing the files, interacting with the user(s), reading and writing files from, and to a disk, and performing other utility functions. Examples of operating systems are MS-DOS, PC-DOS, OS/2, NT, Windows 95, Apple's System 7 Series, NOS, and UNIX. There are other extension programs for graphical and other environments such as Microsoft Windows 3.1, Windows 95, FACE (Framed Access Command Environment) and FMLI (Form and Menu Language Interpreter).

MS-DOS is a single user operating system and only one person may use the system at a time. With Microsoft Windows, you can start up and work with an application software, run more than one application at the same time, transfer information and organize and manage the files you create. These features allow you to perform *multitasking.* Window 95 and OS/2 have multitasking capability.

At this point, I should distinguish between *multitasking* and *multiuser system.* Multitasking allows a single user to perform more than one task at the same time, but a *multiuser* system allows several users each with a separate terminal to simultaneously access the system resources, for example, the UNIX operating system.

Compiler and Language Processor. If you choose to learn a computer language such as C++, or Prolog or LISP, you will need a compiler, which is a program that translates a source program into an executable program (an object program). Some compilers have macrogenerator and language processors. The *language processor* is a functional unit or subprogram that translates and executes computer programs written in a specific programming language for, say, a LISP machine.

LISP Processor (LISP) is a programming language designed for list processing and used extensively for Artificial Intelligence (AI) applications and problems. A LISP machine is a single-user computer designed primarily for the development of AI programs.

Development Tools. Development tools including CASE (Computer Assisted Software Engineering) tools are a set of tools or programs designed to assist programmers in the development of complex applications. Development tools are needed to avoid expensive delays and to improve efficiency of the development process. Development tools allow a prototype system to be developed rapidly so developers can determine earlier in the development process whether a project is feasible or not. For example, in expert system development, development tools include rule definition with error checking capability, parameter specification, context structure definition, interactive structure editor, knowledge base lister and debugging aids. These development tools allow the developer to expedite the construction of a prototype system, thus the term *rapid prototyping*.

Application Programs. An application program is a program that is specific to the solution of an application problem. Normally, it is written for an end-user that performs a service or relates to the user's work. It is sometimes called "productivity software." There are thousands of application programs covering many applications such as accounting, artificial intelligence, database, spreadsheet, word-processing and games. All high-quality application programs are sold with detailed instruction manuals on how to install the software and a user's guide. Very often there is a product support service that you can telephone for help with installing and using the product. The application programs run in concert with the particular operating system.

A Closer Look at the Computer Hardware

The *hardware* consists of the electronic components, boards, peripherals and equipment that make up the physical system as distinguished from programs (software) that instruct the computer hardware what to do. Hardware comes in different system configurations, therefore, we will use several configurations to illustrate the basic components of a modern P.C. The basic hardware of a computer consists of *a system unit, a keyboard and a mouse, a monitor*, connecting cables, and power cables.

The System Unit. The system unit is a metal case that houses the computer internal processing circuitry, including the Central Processing Unit (CPU). The system unit is designed to fit horizontally on the top of a desk or on a small table, a desktop model, see *Figure 5-3*; or a vertical tower model on a desk in a spare corner of a business office, a laboratory, or similar setting. The tower model also is called a floor standing model, see *Figure 5-4*.

On the front panel of a system unit, you may see a power light, diagnostic light, floppy disk(s), a hard disk drive, a reset switch, and a keyboard lock. On the rear (back) panel of a system unit, you may see the power control switch, power receptacle, fan guard, and input/output ports.

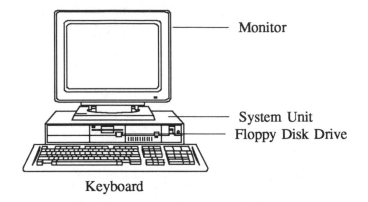

Figure 5-3. Desktop Model of a System Unit

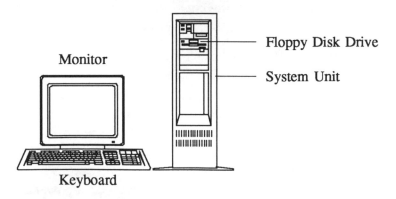

Figure 5-4. Tower Model of a System Unit

The system unit is available in different configurations. To select the right configuration, you must consider the following: type of task to be done on the computer; the volume of work to be processed; the expected transaction or job processing time; the size of the suite of programs to be used on the computer; the size of the files; the transfer rate; and the speed and size of the secondary or auxiliary memory available for that type of system.

Inside the System Unit

If you are a hardware engineer or a qualified technician, and have the schematics and technical manuals for a particular system unit, you may have to open the system unit to perform certain value-added services. The value-added services can include upgrading the memory, say from 8MB to 16MB, installing an adapter card, another floppy disk drive or a peripheral device such as an internal streaming tape (backup tape). Or, you may have to replace a component.

On the other hand, if you are an ordinary user and not a qualified technician, and do not have a technical manual for your computer, then you should only venture inside the case for a quick inspection. You probably will not spend much time observing inside the system unit. However, at a glance, you may observe the following components: circuit boards, microprocessors and chips (miniaturized electronic circuits), memory, and adapters (plug-in boards). But a closer look can reveal other components such as a speaker, controllers for the management of all the integrated and external peripherals, a power supply, floppy disk drive(s), a hard disk drive, cables and connecting wires. Let me describe some important components inside the system unit of a modern PC.

The Microprocessor. The *microprocessor* is the brain of your computer. It is an integrated circuit that contains the Arithmetic and Logical Unit (ALU) and the Control Unit of the Central Processing Unit (CPU). The most popular models of PCs in the United States up to June 30, 1995 used the 486DX2 microprocessor at 66 MHz. These computers are popular in many businesses because they are capable of handling current database queries and report generation adequately. Also, they are used with other devices as a multimedia system for the home or a small office. There are other 486 processors on the market from other semiconductor companies like Advanced Micro Devices (AMD), and Cyrix Corporation.

In 1993 Intel introduced the *Pentium*, a high performance 64-bit microprocessor with two operating modes, a *real address mode* and a *protected mode.*

The real *address mode* supports 1MB memory address space, and the codes are compatible with the 8088, 8086, 80286, 80386 and 80486 processors. A *protected mode*, which supports 4GB of physical memory address space and 64 tera bytes (10^{12}) of virtual memory address space. It also has a four-level memory protection, a built-in memory management unit, and an internal math coprocessor. The speed of the *Pentium* processor can range from 75 MHz to 100 MHz. Personal computers with *pentium* processors cost more than computers with 486DX2 processors. Computer Aided Design users and engineers claim that the extra capability of the Pentium is a distinct advantage in processing their applications. The *Pentium* processor is sometimes called a 586-processor. It has a density of 3.3 million transistors in a single chip including a coprocessor for floating point calculations.

CPU Upgrade. Intel also has an upgrade processor called the *Pentium OverDrive* processor. This processor uses Pentium processor technology to provide improvement in Integer calculations and Floating Points calculations over the performance of the Pentium processor.

However, it is reported that Intel will introduce a new and more powerful processing unit called *P6* with a density of 5.5 million transistors on a single chip. The chip will use a design called a dynamic execution almost like the Reduced Instruction-Set Computer (RISC) design now used in many UNIX workstations. The *P6* is expected to operate at a speed of 133 MHz. This can mean an incredibly powerful PC for desktop applications far beyond what we already have. Very soon we may have to evaluate these computers in terms of millions of instructions per sections (MIPS) as we do with large systems.

The Computer's Memory

The Main Memory - RAM. The memory is the primary storage area of the computer. It stores the instructions, data, the intermediate and final results of the ALU's computations and programs currently executed in RAM. The memory is directly accessible to the CPU. It is known as the primary storage area as distinguished from disk.

The primary storage area or RAM in your computer is known as volatile memory; it does not retain its contents when power to the computer is switched off. Thus, it is a working memory or temporary storage area. When you turn on your computer and run a program and enter data, it is active. But when you turn off the computer, the data that is stored in RAM is lost. For example, if you are editing a file or making changes to it, and want to save the changes permanently, you must save to a permanent medium like a disk before you turn off your computer; else, all the changes made will be lost.

The computer memory is often measured in units of *Kilobytes* or *megabytes*. A byte is the amount of memory that can hold one character of data. In technical terms, it is eight contiguous bits. A kilobyte or 1K is equivalent to 1024 bytes. This unit is conveniently used because the computer architecture is based on binary numbers. Bytes are counted in powers of two; thus 1024 is close to 1000 therefore, the word, *kilo*. And, one megabyte or 1MB is equivalent to 1048576 bytes. Also, some software require a certain amount of RAM, or Random Access Memory to work properly. For example, to use WordPerfect for Windows in the Windows environment, you will need a minimum of 4MB of RAM to work comfortably. Some software programs use a large amount of RAM especially when using graphics, so a system with 8MB of RAM is required for most desktop processing.

Read Only Memory (ROM). This is a part of the main memory of a modern computer. ROM contains essential system programs and subroutines written in binary code that are electrically embedded or frozen at the factory to store the instructions permanently in the memory. The instructions enable the computer to operate smoothly, such as checking for hardware problems when you first switch on your computer. The instructions also enable the computer to look for a disk, control the monitor, keyboard, mouse and for configuration information. ROM is not *volatile* and does not need to be refreshed with periodic electronic signals. Also, the content of a ROM is not lost when the computer is shutdown and the power is switched off.

Cache Memory. This is a special buffer section, which is smaller and faster than the main memory that is set aside to hold a copy of instructions and data in main memory that are likely to be needed next by the processor. This section is controlled by a cache controller chip, which improves the speed of a computer because the microprocessor does not have to wait for the slower dynamic random access memory (DRAM) chips to catch up. With a cache memory, a microprocessor can operate at zero wait state.

Basic Input-Output System (BIOS)

The Basic Input-Output System (BIOS) is an important program that is electrically embedded in Read Only Memory (ROM) in the IBM PC-Compatible computers. The BIOS contains coded instructions and routines for supporting the transfer of information between various elements of the system, such as the memory, the disk drive, keyboard, display, other peripherals.

The BIOS of IBM personal computers and Personal System/2 (PS/2) is the copyright of IBM. However, some IBM PC-Compatible manufacturers use BIOS from such companies, Phoenix Technologies and American Megatrends Inc. (AMI). The BIOS also has a version number. A larger version number signifies a later product release. Thus, a later release shows product improvement of some kind. So it is possible that a BIOS with a low version may have difficulty running certain software.

Bus

The bus is an internal pathway along which signals are transmitted from one part or device of the computer to another. In personal computers, the bus in designed with three pathways, data bus, address bus, and control bus.

The bus structure is closely related to the architecture of the computer, and there are many types of bus structure. For example, some Apple Macintosh computers use the NuBus while the popular

IBM AT and compatibles use an Industry Standard Architecture (ISA) bus with 8/16 bits data path. Also, in 1987, IBM introduced its Micro Channel 32-bit Architecture (MCA) for its PS/2 computers, and shortly after the introduction of MCA, a consortium of computers introduced an Extended Industry Standard Architecture (EISA) 32-bit bus with a compatible mode to the ISA bus. Then recently Intel introduced the Peripheral Component Interconnect (PCI) bus. This bus enhances system performance by increasing the speed and throughput of signals for graphics and communications applications.

The result of all the different bus structures is that either you have a computer with one type of bus structure such as a NuBus or MCA Bus, or, build a hybrid PC that contains both an ISA bus and a PCI bus with compatibility in mind. This is particularly important if you are still running software written with ISA structure in mind. You also can have a computer with ISA bus and EISA slots for certain applications.

Secondary Storage: Four Types of Media

This is a nonvolatile storage medium. It stores programs and data even when the computer is switched off. This term is synonymous with auxiliary storage. Four types of media may be used for storing programs and data.

The first is *floppy disk*. A floppy disk is a removable medium, and except for LAN or an on-line connection to a multiuser system, floppy disks are the usual way in which programs and text files are communicated from one computer to another. A modern computer comes with an 3.5", 1.44MB floppy disk drive as standard (Drive A:). A 2.88MB optional floppy disk drive is now available. Depending upon your particular configuration, a 5.25 inch, 1.2MB Floppy Disk Drive (Drive B:) can be added.

The second type of secondary storage medium is a *hard disk*, sometimes called fixed disk. This is a complex storage subsystem that includes the disks, cylinders the read/write head assembly, and the electronic interface that governs the connection between the drive and the computer. The access time and the capacity of hard disk drive are important. The typical 486DX2 computer comes either 420MB or 540MB hard disk, although some personal computers can have in them as much as 2 GB hard drive.

The third type of secondary storage medium is a *tape backup unit*. This secondary storage medium is designed to backup onto magnetic cartridge all the data on a hard disk at high speeds. The magnetic tape cartridge is a removable storage device, and the modern ones are smaller than the DC300XLP cartridge.

And, the fourth type of secondary storage for PC is a removable drive and media. An example is an IOMEGA ZIP Drive with a 100 MG removable disk. Also, there are rewritable optical disk with optical media for use as back-up for your software.

CD-ROM Drive

In the modern PC, it is likely that your computer will come with a CD-ROM Drive, with a double-speed 300 KB/second transfer rate or quadruple-speed to improve viewing of video for Windows and quick time multimedia presentation. You will need the appropriate disk (for DOS or Windows) to make the system work. Originally, Compact Disk (CD) were designed to record digital music tracks. The computer industry adopted the CD as a way of storing large digital files, but to conform to the computer terminology the industry decided to call them CD-ROM.

FAX MODEM

The modern PC may have an internal FAX MODEM that fits into one of the bus slots. The current series has a data transmission rate of 14400 bps (14.4 bits per second), a 14400 group 3 send/receive FAX and throughput up to 57600 bps utilizing V.42 and MNP5 data compression.

This is a full-featured MODEM that enables the PC to communicate via telephone line with other computers, terminals, or timesharing systems. It also has a send/receive FAX function that makes and terminates calls, manages the communication session, transmits and receives image data. A facsimile (FAX) is a device that transmits and receives images and text on paper.

The Keyboard

The keyboard is an input device that allows you to communicate with the computer by entering characters, data, commands and instructions. You use the keyboard to input instructions and make the operating system or application programs do work for you. In some modern computers, you have to turn the keyboard key to the unlocked position before you can use it. The keyboard key-lock is there to prevent unauthorized use of the computer. By engaging the lock with a key and removing the key, you cannot use the keyboard, thus, preventing an unauthorized user from using the system.

There are many types of keyboards. On the IBM, PCXT and compatibles, there is the standard keyboard. On the PS/2 Personal computers, there is the extended or "enhanced" keyboard, known as 101-keyboard, and there is a 102 keyboard with a detachable unit. In this Chapter, we will describe the popular 101-keyboard.

Keyboard Sections

The 101-Keyboard has three sections. Each of these sections contains keys with special meaning to the computer system. The three sections are the function keys, the alphanumeric section and numeric keypad section.

Function Keys. They consist of a group of ten keys located on the left-hand side of the standard keyboard, or a group of twelve keys at the top of the enhanced keyboard. What function keys are used for depends on the software or application being used. For example, MS-DOS6 uses F1 to display Help information on your screen. In another software, a different function may be assigned to F1.

The Alphanumeric Section. The Alphanumeric section is the main section of the keyboard. It contains all the letter keys, punctuation keys, and spacebar, and resembles or works like the keys on a typewriter.

The Numeric Keypad Section. The numeric keys on the right-hand side of the keyboard are grouped together or set up to resemble the keypad on an adding machine of a calculator. The keypad is a quick and easy way to enter numbers, particularly if you are used to using adding machines and calculators.

   To use the numeric keypad, you must press the **Num Lock** key. The indicator light on the top right-hand side of the keyboard will come on. The keyboard works like the **Caps Lock** on your typewriter. To turn the numeric keypad off, you press the **Num Lock** key again and the indicator light will go off. Also, you should remember that you also can use the keys in the upper row of the alpha numeric section to enter numbers into your computer, if you wish.

Esc or Escape Key. The **Esc** or **Escape** key appears on the upper left corner of the keyboard. The use of the Esc key depends on the software or application being used. Often, it is used to return to the preceding menu.

Ctrl or Control Key. The **Ctrl** key is used with other keys. The use of the **Ctrl** key depends on the software or application. However, by holding down the **Ctrl** key and the **Alt** key while pressing the **Delete** key <**Ctrl+Alt+Del**>, you can reboot the system from the keyboard.

Alt or Alternate Key. The **Alt** key is often used with another key such as the **Ctrl** key in the example shown above. However, when using MS-DOSSHELL, you can press the **Alt** key to select a menu bar.

The Backspace Key. The **Backspace** key (←) is used to delete the character to the left of the cursor.

The Enter Key. The **Enter** key is used to complete an entry, and tell MS-DOS6 to proceed with what you have typed on the current line. It also does a Carriage Return. That is, it moves the cursor down one line, or moves it over to the beginning of a new line.

The Arrow Keys. The use of the **Arrow** keys depends on the software application you are using. Usually, the arrow keys help you to move around the screen as indicated by the arrow. On the standard keyboard the arrow keys are located on the numeric keypad with the numbers. But, on the enhanced keyboard, the arrow keys are located to the lower left of the numeric keypad. You can use the arrow keys on the enhanced keyboard anytime without having to make sure the **Num Lock** is not turned on nor active, as with the standard keyboard. When you press an arrow key, it moves the cursor one character either to the left or right or one line up or down as indicated by the direction of the arrow.

Shift and Caps Lock Keys. The **Shift** and **Caps Lock** keys are part of the alphanumeric section. The use of the **Shift** key depends on the software or application you are using. Usually, when you press the **Shift** key and type a character, you get an uppercase (letter) character. You also can enter uppercase letters or capital letters by pressing the **Caps Lock** key. Once this key is pressed, an indicator light comes on at the top right-hand side of the enhanced keyboard or on the **Caps Lock** key itself. It indicates that the alphanumeric section of the keyboard is in the upper case letter mode. But, if you want to return to the lowercase letter mode, press the **Caps Lock** key again, and the indicator light will go off.

The Monitor or Display

A monitor is an output device that produces a television-like on-screen display, the primary means of presenting information to a computer user. A monitor also is called a Visual Display Unit (VDU) or a CRT, the acronym for the Cathode-Ray Tube. The sharpness of the image and the capacity of information that can be displayed depends on the "resolution" of the screen, and its ability to display what is produced out of a video output circuitry. This is an important measurement of information as propounded by Wiener N. (1948) in his book, "Cybernetics of Control and Communication in the Animal and the Machine." Also, propounded by Shannon, C., and Weaver, W., (1949), in "The Mathematical Theory of Communication," Urbana, University of Illinois Press.

The resolution is the number of *pixels* or dots, or picture elements per inch a video screen can display. The total number of horizontal and vertical pixels a screen can display will determine whether a monitor is high or low resolution.

Digital and Analog Monitors. There are digital monitors and analog monitors. Digital monitors are fast and can produce sharp images and text. But, they are limited by a prearranged standard such as an IBM Monochrome Display Adapter or a Hercules Graphic Adapter. A monochrome monitor displays one color against a black or white background, but it can have a green or amber image.

A digital color Monitor can display sharp images and text with the use of a Color Graphic Adapter (CGA) or Enhanced Graphic Adapter (EGA). But, it cannot display continuous variable signals. To take advantage of this limitation, some manufacturers have produced color monitors that can be adapted to various frequencies so they can be used with different adapters. Some of these monitors can be switched from a digital mode to an analog mode, and vice versa.

VGA Monitors. An analog monitor can display continuous-varied colors and a Video Graphics Array (VGA) with as many as 256 continuous variable colors simultaneously with a resolution of 640 by 480 pixels. This is known as a *bit-mapped* display. A bit-map is a representation of a video image stored in memory. A bit-mapped display holds space in a memory to control each pixel or picture element on the screen individually. While in operation, the computer redraws or "refreshes" the entire image on the screen continuously, and when representing color and shades of gray, the computer assigns more than one bit to a pixel. There is a look-up table that conveys information about the value of the bits assigned to each pixel.

Improvement in the resolution and the design of monitors is taking place. Some monitors have 1024 by 768 pixels with up to 256 colors displayed simultaneously, anti-static screen, reduced magnetic field and are ergonomically designed. There are Super Video Graphic Array (SVGA) monitors with 800 x 600 and 256 colors and Extended VGA with 1024 x 768 resolution. However, you cannot achieve such high resolution without the proper video graphic adapter (card). The Video adapter card determines the actual screen resolutions and number of colors your monitor can display.

Additional Hardware Devices

Besides the basic units of a computer, there are other peripheral devices that you may want to include to make your computer system more versatile. These additional devices are: a mouse, a printer, and a set of an amplified computer stereo sound speakers to work with your CD-ROM subsystem. Remember that you have to install a high quality sound card or voice audio card that produces CD-quality sound and music through your computer.

A Mouse

A *mouse* is an input device equipped with two or more control buttons housed in a case designed to fit under your hand. See *Figure 5-5*. The mouse is moved about on the table next to the keyboard. As the mouse moves on your desk, its circuits relay signals that cause an on-screen pointer to move accordingly. The on-screen pointer is shaped like an arrow, but it can take different shape when using certain programs.

A mouse is best used with graphics, icons and windows. In a graphical environment, if you have a menu on your screen and want to select an item from that menu, all you have to do is to move the mouse until the tip of the arrow rests on or point to what you want, then **click.** In other words, press and quickly release the mouse button. You can **double-click** by clicking the mouse button twice in rapid succession. You can **drag** by holding down the mouse button while moving the mouse. People who use mice believe that a mouse makes the computer easier to use. This is particularly evident when using a graphical user interface (GUI).

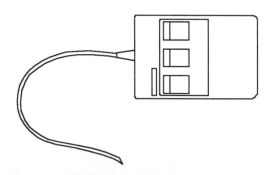

Figure 5-5. Three Button Mouse

A mouse may be connected to the computer in one of the following ways:

1. Through an adapter board, which fits into an expansion slot on the system board. Some video (adapter) boards have a mouse port and a video port. The type of mouse that connects into an adapter board is called a bus mouse.
2. A mouse can be used by connecting it to a standard serial port. This type of mouse is called a serial mouse.
3. Also a mouse may be connected through a special mouse port that is built into the system unit or to the keyboard of a terminal.

Mouse Driver. A mouse is of little use to you without a software program known as a *mouse driver*. A mouse driver is software that you load into the system. It contains the interface instructions that let the mouse communicate with your screen and your application. Information from the mouse, the screen, and your application work together.

The right mouse programs allow you fast and visual access to programs and files in a MS-DOS6.22 and Windows environment.

Printers

A printer is an output device that converts data or information that has been processed onto paper. There are many kinds, and different brands of printers. To simplify our discussion we will classify them into two groups: impact printers and non-impact printers.

Impact Printers. Impact printers form an image or character by striking the inked ribbon, paper and platen by a print wire, or by a hammer into a daisy wheel or print thimble, to form an impression on the page. "Dot-Matrix" printers and "Letter-Quality" printers are examples of impact printers.

Dot Matrix Printers. A dot-matrix printer is a highly integrated device with its own microprocessor and complex electro/mechanical components. Dot-matrix printers are fast. The speed varies from 120 characters per second (cps) to 400 cps. The quality also varies from poor (characters not fully formed) to acceptable. Many dot-matrix printers have a Near Letter Quality (NLQ) mode that gives up speed to produce improved output. These printers can have either a 9-pin print head, an 18-pin print head, or a 24-pin print-head.

Generally, a 24-wire (pin) print head has finer quality, and prints better than a printer with a 9-pin print head. The modern dot matrix printer has some resident print fonts, such as Letter-Gothic 20cpi, Elite (NLQ) 12cpi, Pica 10, High Speed 12, Courier 72, Bold and Proportional Spacing. It also allows programmable fonts. Dot matrix printers can be noisy, but they are flexible in that they can use 3 or 4 part forms, and can produce both text and graphic output. Also, they are somewhat cheaper than other printers. A diagram of an impact printer using continuous forms is presented in *Figure 5-6.*

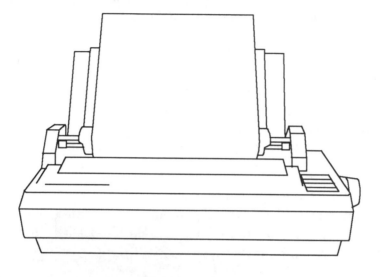

Figure 5-6. A Diagram of an Impact Printer

Letter Quality Printers. A Letter-Quality Printer is an impact printer that uses a highly-integrated microprocessor and modern electronics to drive and position a print hammer to strike a type element. The print element or daisy wheel or print thimble rotates quickly against the inked ribbon, paper and platen. The operation produces fully formed text characters much like a high quality office typewriter, and at speeds ranging from 20 cps to 55cps.

A letter-Quality printer is slower than a dot-matrix printer, but produces a higher quality printing. One can change a print font by simply changing the type element or daisy wheel or print thimble. A letter-quality printer does not produce graphic images, and is more suitable for text and word processing. It can accept plain office paper like a typewriter or continuous paper with a pin-feed tractor. It can handle multiple copies, but makes a certain amount of noise (like a typewriter) during its operations.

Non-Impact Printers. Non-impact printers use different methods for producing text and graphic output on paper. For example, Hewlett-

Packard's "ink jet" and "paint jet" printers use a method of spraying ink from a matrix of very small jets and thermal ink jets, to produce text and graphics. Laser printers and other page printers use laser beam and Light-Emitting Diode (LED) technology to produce text and graphic output on paper, at 300 dpi, and at a rate of six or eight pages per minute, or even faster.

Page Printers. Notice that when we discussed impact printers, we often used characters per second (cps) when referring to the speed of a printer. But, with nonimpact printers we use pages per minute to measure the print speed of these printers. Many nonimpact printers use laser beam scanning and electrophotography to produce output on paper at 300 dpi, thus earning the name "laser printers." But, there are printers that use other technologies, such as Light-Emitting Diode (LED) technology and electrophotography to produce output on paper at 300 dpi. The implication is that not all such nonimpact printers use laser beam. Perhaps a more accurate name for such printers should be "page printers" We will use the term "page printers" to include laser printers and printers using LED technologies. *Figure 5-7* shows a pictorial representation of a page printer.

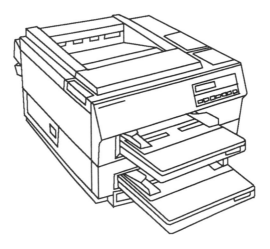

Figure 5-7. Page Printer (Laser Printer)

Page printers can produce sharp graphics' images and drawings from programs. They can produce more images and typefaces than an impact printer. They are faster and quieter than an impact printer, but cost more. There are a variety of page printers; some use additional electronic boards and special toners to boost or increase the resolution to 800 x 800 dpi or 1000 x 1000 dpi. Some page printers are faster, and use all-points-addressable (APA) mode, which allows the use of multiple fonts per page on any variety of available size of forms. Others use a "Postscript" language that describes how to print a page that blends text and graphics.

Postscript is a programming language promoted by Adobe Systems Inc. This is a special programming language, unlike PASCAL, FORTRAN or COBOL. It is designed specially for generating codes to describe an image of a page, and how to print a page that has a mixture of text and graphics. An application program that has a Postscript printer driver will generate these codes accordingly, and the user will not have to worry how the computer does the task.

Setting Up Your Computer System

Before you connect or set up your computer system, you should first select a suitable site for your computer. There should be site planning and you should consider ergonomic factors to achieve a level of comfort and maximum efficiency. Here are some guidelines:

Locate a clean and dust free area that offers a stable surface. There should be proper lighting, and adequate ventilation. The computer should be separated from large electrical motors, or radio and TV transmitters. These devices can give out to avoid strong electromagnetic fields, which can interfere with the operations of your computer. Use comfortable chairs, and make sure that you follow proper building regulations and safety standards.

Connecting Your System

The keyboard has a connector that must be plugged into a socket at the back panel of the system unit. The system unit needs an AC power cord. The female end of the power cord plugs into the back of the system unit, and the three-pronged (male) end plugs into a surge suppressor or a grounded power outlet.

Connecting the Monitor

The monitor is connected by a signal cable that has a video input connector at one end, which is plugged into the video adapter at the back panel of the system unit. The other end of the signal cable goes to the monitor and may be fixed permanently to the monitor. The monitor needs an AC power cable, one end (the female end) plugs in the socket on the rear of the monitor. The other end (the three-pronged) male plug fits into either a convenient power outlet on the back panel of the system unit, a power outlet of a surge suppressor, or a grounded power outlet.

Figure 5-8. A Desktop Computer on a Clear Working Environment

After you have connected the peripheral devices to your system unit, switch on the computer by pressing the ON/OFF switch to ON. The monitor also has an ON/OFF switch; press the ON switch. When the system is switched ON, a series of auto-diagnostic tests is executed to check that the basic components and attached peripheral devices are working properly. The system beeps once after the tests are successfully completed. The floppy drive will flash, and if there is no bootable disk in drive A, the computer will load the CONFIG.SYS File and your AUTOEXEC.BAT Files from your hard disk into memory. Depending on the brand of your computer, there should be a welcome message and menu, a list of options displayed on screen to the user from which the user can select an action to be initiated.

Questions for Discussion and Review

1. Define the term system. What is a Cybernetic system?

2. Draw a block diagram for a teaching/learning system using the concept of *feedback*. And, explain this diagram to your class.

3. Describe two input devices of the modern PC or workstation. Explain how they are used.

4. "A computer system should be looked at as an organized whole, not just at a particular Hardware." Discuss.

5. Define the following terms:

   Port
   Boot
   Video graphics adapter

High resolution
Monochrome monitor

6. State seven major hardware components of a computer. Describe each briefly.

7. Describe the following terms:

    CD-ROM
    FAX-MODEM
    BUS
    Cache Memory
    Operating System

8. What is RAM? Explain the statement, "RAM is *Volatile* as compared with secondary memory." Give an example.

9. Answer the following questions briefly.

    What is a postscript printer?
    What is a letter quality printer?
    What is a dot-matrix printer?

10. Describe the following:

    Language Processor
    Development Tools
    LISP
    Rapid Prototyping

Chapter 6

Computers in Education

The subject of computers in education requires some philosophical distinctions between the educational goods in terms of education and the services computer provide in a college or university. From a linguistic point of view we should be clear about what computers in education means.

Education is the process of imparting knowledge or skill by systematic instruction. This involves an increase in human rationality and understanding in different kinds of knowledge that are acquired through teaching and learning. Is a person who works in the computer center on students enrollment or the consultant that goes around with a laptop computer to the chancellor's office of a community college district advising on how to recruit the next president involved in education?

These two activities may be providing interesting services for the education institution or education system, but cannot be regarded as pertaining to education. For not everything that goes on in an educational institution is education. Therefore, from the linguistic point of view, we must be clear what education means.

If a person studies or conducts research in the process of learning about computers or the computer as a subject for study, with an eye on the educational goods of students developing an understanding of computers, this is a study in education. Whereas if a person is studying the computing services that are necessary in a modern college or university, the person must define those services and distinguish them from the use of computers in research, and in the teaching/learning situation.

Moreover, if we include the type of consultant describe above with the student counselor, day care unit, campus police and other general services, then the term "education" would be misused. Also, if we define everything that goes on in an educational institution as education, then we cannot differentiate which services are directly related to education, administration and so forth, and how effective each service is, and how much it costs.

The Computer as a Subject of Study

From the contents of Chapters 2, 3, 4 and 5, it is obvious that these topics treat computers as a subject of study intended for students and readers to become computer literate or to improve their understanding of computers, at least in a general way. In fact, many private and public colleges are offering computer courses. Students of all disciplines need to know about computers as a general educational requirement or should attend classes on computer literacy. Colleges or universities that fail to offer such courses are placing their students at a disadvantage in future years and will reduce their chances in the job market.

Now, let us discuss briefly three kinds computing services that are necessary in a college or university. These services are: Administrative Computing, Research Computing and Instructional Computing.

Administrative Computing

Administrative computing supports the business operations of the university or college. It includes admissions and registration, payroll, accounting, scheduling, student accounts receivable, personnel records, library, institutional studies and other functions. The administrative computer system also supports the information processing activity that generates the various reports that must be filed to State and Federal agencies. Moreover, the administrative computer system must be reliable and secure.

The administrative computer system must be up and running, and its ability to perform the required functions under stated conditions for a stated period should be relied upon. It must not be "down" when processing the payroll or vendors checks, otherwise, employees and vendors will not be paid on time. Also, the administrative computer system must be a "Trusted Computing Base (TCB) System." The system should be secured throughout its life-cycle. Students and faculty should not be allowed to access this system. The hardware and software themselves also should be protected against unauthorized changes that could cause the security mechanism to malfunction or be bypassed completely.

Research Computing

Research computing supports faculty research, organized research, and graduate programs. The type of research usually involves an investigation or inquiry to gather new information or to collate what is already known about a field of discipline or subject, especially as a scholarly or scientific pursuit. Research computing fulfills a different function from data processing and information processing systems describe above.

Research computing supports faculty research. It is very likely that this function may involve the acquisition of supercomputers, mainframe computers, minicomputers and PCs linked in networks. These are very expensive hardware systems, which are sometimes augmented by requests from faculty in the sciences, engineering and social sciences for software, new terminals, and upgrades to maintain a state-of-the-art system. Besides, these expensive computer systems may be housed in a separate building called the "computer center."

Some computer centers have their own conference rooms, high-tech classroom laboratories and own faculty members and staff payroll. If your university is planning to become a major player in engineering, scientific or medical research, then the need to acquire or have access to a mainframe or supercomputers may be real. This is particularly true, if there are sufficient requests for computer resources from faculty in their grants and contract proposals to secure funding from outside agencies.

Instructional Computing

Instructional computing involves the use of the computer as a tool in the educational process. It can be used by the instructor in the classroom and by students who interact directly with the computer. The computer can bring to education such attributes as unending patience, individuals and student-paced instruction programs. Computer programs such as Computer-Assisted Instruction (CAI) and other computer-based educational programs play an important part in the process of education.

With Computer-Assisted Instruction, the interested student sits at a terminal or in front of his microcomputer with a prescribed program loaded in memory. The computer presents instructional information and questions; the student studies the information and instruction presented on the screen then interacts with the computer by either answering questions, or asking questions of his or her own. Depending on the topic, the interaction can take one or more combinations of teaching methods such as drill-and-practice, tutoring, inquiry, dialogue, problem solving, games, and simulation. The computer accepts, or analyzes the responses, then provides immediate feedback to the student's responses, and maintains a record of the student's performance.

CAI is useful in areas of mathematics, physics, statistics, spelling and languages. Also, it provides individualized help to a student who may be slow or too shy to ask questions or provide help to a student who wants to progress faster without being constrained by slower learners. An important developer of a successful CAI system was Donald Bitzer at the University of Illinois, Urbana. He and others developed the CDC PLATO system.

In the last fifteen years, colleges and universities have spent large sums of money on computers to improve faculty productivity and increase the quality of instruction. But the key question remains, what is the impact of computers on *pedagogy*? Let us discuss this question and show how computers may and may not be used in a teaching/learning situation.

The Impact of Computers on Pedagogy

In the case of *pedagogy* - the art of teaching - many colleges and universities that rush to buy PCs for their classrooms cannot prove that these PCs influence the art of teaching. In fact, their instructional process remains largely the same. This is in contrast with other sectors of our society where computers and information technology have changed the way business is transacted, how airline reservations are made, how airplanes are designed, and how certain medical problems are diagnosed. When examining the role of computers in the teaching/learning situation in many colleges and universities, it is not difficult to understand that computers have not always achieved their professed goals.

Computers and technology are not the panaceas for all educational problems including teaching and learning. Nevertheless, they can play an invaluable role in the teaching/learning situation, and in the delivery of education and training to meet varied needs. However, before we go into our discussion about how computers and information technology can influence the art of teaching or help in a teaching/learning situation, we need to identify some important obstacles, and examine them briefly.

Some Obstacles

Lack of Philosophical Analysis. The first obstacle towards integrating computer and information technology with teaching and learning is a lack of philosophical analysis as to the purpose of teaching. This goes to the root of the question, what is an instructor or a professor? What does instructing entail?

An instructor or professor is a person directly engaged in instructing a group of students on a specific topic during a period. An instructor is a member of the faculty or teaching staff with regular teaching functions. This definition includes professors, who are teachers of high rank.

Purposeful (Teleological) Behavior. The term "purposeful" is meant "to denote that the act of behavior may be interpreted as directed to the attainment of a goal, i.e., to a final condition in which the behaving object reaches a definite correlation in time or in space with respect to another object or event," Rosenblueth, Wiener and Bigelow (1943). We need to ask the following: What do we expect an instructor to accomplish? Is it to disseminate information and handouts? Is it to provide a framework for reading? Is it to promote thought? Is it to generate interest in the subject being taught? Is it to provide the necessary information when satisfactory textbooks and illustrations are lacking? A philosophical analysis will help to *clarify* the meaning of these questions. Philosophy is not just concerned with what is the case, but how to make what is the case, more like what *ought to* be the case.

In answer to the question what does instructing entail, we can say instruction entails cognitive studies, programmed instructions, theories of instruction and learning, and feedback. A theory or method of instruction should be *prescriptive* in that it should set the criteria and state the conditions for improving learning. It should specify how the information is to be organized as a whole, and how the body of knowledge should be structured so the learner can comprehend it. It should specify the most effective sequences in which to present the information and forms of knowledge to be learned.

The instructor must be able to have knowledge of results and know how well he or she has taught the subject. Besides feedback, the instructor should know what degree of difficulty is likely to be met with the use of computers or information technology, and how this difficulty can be overcome.

Lack of Training in Instructional and Learning Theories. In many professions, such as airline pilots, registered nurses or bus drivers, a recruit with no previous experience must undertake training. The recruit must learn certain rules, everyday skills, what bad habits he or she should get rid of, and what dangers can occur if these rules and skills are not put into practice.

Unfortunately, in many colleges and universities, a new instructor with no previous teaching experience is entrusted by the chairperson or head of a department with the teaching of students, even in a field of discipline that he has not majored in, or with no practical experience in the subject matter. The instructor or professor may not know what an instructor is supposed to accomplish, nor the various ways, least of all the best way of getting the students to learn what he/she has to teach. It is time for a reform of the regular teaching functions in higher education.

Lack of Training in How to Teach with Computers and Technology. Another obstacle toward integrating computers and information technology in the instructional process in colleges and universities is a lack of training in how to teach with computers and technology. The emphasis on putting more computers in colleges and constructing high-tech classrooms without seriously considering training for the instructors is wrong. Learning about computers is different from learning how to use computers and information technology in the instructional process.

With a lack of training, many dedicated instructors are left on their own to explore new ways of using computers and technology in their instructional process. However, there is a danger in this do-it-yourself approach. An instructor with no training or knowledge of theories of instruction and learning can become so fascinated with computers, multimedia images, pretty pictures, getting students to communicating on the *internet* with others worldwide that he can lose sight of the subject he is paid to teach. Thus, fascination for computers and technology is not enough; it is how this technology can fit the instructor's perspective in the teaching/learning situation in a formal college or university setting that is of primary importance.

People are Looking to Computers and Technology for Educational and Economic Solutions

Around the world, including developing countries, people are looking to computers and technology to help them learn, as their own goals change along with economic conditions. Educators, dedicated teachers, instructors and professors also are looking to computers and technology to transform the teaching/learning situations in schools and higher education.

Besides these groups, people outside the traditional colleges and universities are looking to computers and technology to provide alternatives to conventional higher educational institutions that are becoming more expensive and inconvenient. New organizations are entering the education and training market. They are going to bring *accredited* information, knowledge and courses to the learner at home or wherever he wishes it to be, via computer and information technology.

Computers and information technology in education have the potential to correct deficiencies in basic skills, reinforce skills, augment teaching and learning, and improve the delivery and distribution of information and knowledge. Their potential is enormous, but good management and careful thinking are needed for this potential to come into being. Let us take a brief look at some things mentioned in this paragraph in which computers and information technology can make a difference.

Computers Can Help in Remedial Education

It is not unusual in the United States of America to find students with high school diplomas that are deficient in basic skills. Their reading and writing skills can be as low as sixth grade level, and their mathematical skills are well below eighth grade level. If for one reason or another, one of these students becomes infused with a strong desire to return to college or take a vocational course, then he can soon find himself at a disadvantage when he goes to a community or another college.

Often cited as the reasons for the disadvantage are: the student is a poor single parent with children to care for, or the student had to "drop out" of high school for personal, family and economic reasons, or the student is a poor immigrant from another country where

English is not the primary language. But the logical reason is that these students are not prepared for academic work because they are deficient in the basic skills of reading, writing and mathematics.

The likely effects of this situation are that these students may find it difficult to follow the main classroom teaching/learning situations or to complete the exercises in the "math lab" with the rest of students that possess basic literacy skills. Under these circumstances, disadvantaged students are likely to "drop out" from the college or be encouraged to "tag along," although their performance is well below the satisfactory grade, particularly, when enrollment figures and class size are emphasized. Instead of tacitly encouraging mediocrity or a "revolving door" situation, and, passing these deficient students onto industry, business, government or to another college or university, instructors and administrators ought to take a page out of modern management literature, and implement the Total Quality Management (TQM) concept in their colleges.

A Computer-Based Education Laboratory

Computers and information technology can be used to mitigate these deficiencies and even improve the quality of students by reinforcing certain skills taught in the traditional classroom setting. The mechanism by which this is done is described as a computer-based education laboratory.

The Computer-Based Education (CBE) Laboratory's priority is to improve basic skills in reading, writing and mathematics as a remedial education function that can help to solve this problem. It should include individualized computer-assisted instructions, a user-friendly interface, ergonomically designed hardware and work environment, courseware (educational materials) and qualified tutors. It also should be concerned with quality and improvement.

Concerned faculty members from the English language department who teach general reading, writing skills, and from the Mathematics department who teach basic mathematics courses to the general body of students should identify the software programs that will help remedial students. These faculty members should be given a certain amount of teaching research credit for evaluating relevant educational software, customizing it, and testing it on new students who are deficient in certain basic skills.

The college should give a *pretest* for literacy to new students enrolled for college preparation courses. If the test results show deficiencies in certain basic skills, those students affected should be directed to take appropriate remedial course in the CBE Laboratory. The particular course of instructions will be prescribed and monitored by one or more concerned faculty members described in the above paragraph.

The responsibility for monitoring the students and their progress in the computer-assisted instructions laboratory should not be delegated to a young student assistant who likes to fiddle around with computers. The main reason is that monitoring students and correcting their deficiencies requires serious educational and professional commitments, and are too important to be entrusted to a student assistant who just likes to fiddle with computers.

The instructors responsible for correcting students' deficiencies in basic literacy skills must understand the following: how to motivate these students to correct their deficiencies; how to coordinate the remedial computer-assisted instructions with the text books and subjects that are being taught in the general classroom; and, how to use the information and knowledge gained to improve the quality of education.

A computer-based education laboratory for developing basic literacy skills and providing remedial education to deficient students is an important alternative to a high college "drop out" rate, or to passing deficient students on to business, industry and government. Deficient students need time and patience to get them up to a satisfactory level. At the CBE Laboratory students can get personalized one-to-one computer-assisted instruction where they have to interact immediately. Some students require much more time to complete certain drills-and-practice, problem solving, and get through certain exercises. With a computer-assisted learning environment, the student can work at his or her own pace or take more time without worrying about keeping other students waiting. Also, some adults that have deficiencies in basic literacy skills are sometimes embarrassed and do not want to reveal their shortcomings in a group situation, and will do their best to conceal their deficiency, even to the extent of dropping out of class. But with the CBE Laboratory no one except the tutor (or instructor) knows what their shortcomings are.

When the student achieves proficiency in basic literacy skills he or she will be given a *post-test* or exit test out of the remedial program and will continue with the main body of students (See *Figure 6-1* TOTE Diagram). The positive side of such a program is that the college would play a functional role in overcoming the student's academic deficiency, reduce "drop outs," improve the quality of the person and his or her capability to complete a college education.

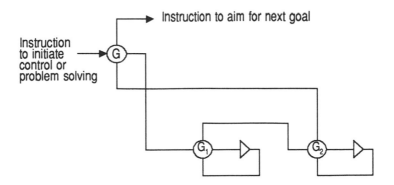

Figure 6-1. TOTE Diagram

CAI Can Re-Enforce Skills

Computer-assisted Instruction synonymous with *Computer-Aided Instruction* (CAI) is the use of computer-based instructional programs to perform instructional tasks, such as drill and practice, tutorials, and tests. Unlike human instructors, a CAI program does not get bored or frustrated with slow students, nor make distinctions of gender and race. A modern CAI program can use sound graphics, animation, text, and on-screen rewards to engage the student in learning.

Computer-assisted instructions can strengthen the quality of a student by offering additional educational materials in many subjects that are taught in the classroom. For example, PLATO, a multimedia computer-based educational delivery system, and other reputable educational software companies offer a variety of programs that faculty members can use to reinforce certain skills that are part of the subject they are teaching in the classroom. These programs may be self-paced tutorials with many independent modules or lessons which faculty members can choose to support their text books or class discussions.

Multimedia Systems for Teaching Foreign Languages

A multimedia system is a system capable of presenting multimedia materials in its entirety. The term *multimedia* refers to the presentation of information on a computer using a combination of text, graphics, video, animation and sound.

Some developers use digitized images on computers and link their system to a Video Disk Player with a color monitor or a television screen to give students audio/visual and movement while using a computer-based program. One such program is *Philippe*, which was developed by Gilberte Furstenberg and Janet Murray at the Massachusetts Institute of Technology to teach French and French culture. Dartmouth College also uses software including digitized pronunciation by native speakers and multimedia system with CD-ROM, audio, video computer, and telecommunication capabilities in their language resource center.

Computer-based Technology Can Augment Traditional Teaching Methods

Computer technology can make the teaching/learning situation more interesting, and it can increase the productivity of the instructor or teacher. It also can yield favorable results in the following cases: where the curriculum for a discipline was designed thirty or forty years ago, but changed only slightly over the years, and text books lack adequate illustrations; and where tenured faculty members continue to use their old lecture notes in the traditional lecture-text-book-homework format.

The use of computer technology with multimedia graphical illustrations also can liven up the teaching/learning situation and generate students' interest in the subject. However, Instructors may have to change their lecture format and revise their old lecture notes. This change can give the instructor a fresh look at his subject. Take the subject of Physics. The instructor can build different illustrations, designs, simulated motions around a particular concept. He or she can provide experiments where each student can interact with the computer to measure the behavior of an object and noting such characteristics as motion and speed. Motivated and intelligent honor's students can explore certain possibilities and answer certain questions themselves.

With computer technology, an instructor can construct valid up-to-date illustrations of technical concepts to augment limited illustrations in textbooks. This type of teaching method encourages students to interact, ask questions and generate interest in the subject. Without getting into a debate on whether students will learn the subject more thoroughly with the use of computer technology than without, there are sufficient educational reasons for teachers and instructors to have a positive approach to computers in teaching.

Computers and Information Technology Can Improve the Delivery and Distribution of Knowledge and Education

Since the Open University in Great Britain in 1971 began offering academic opportunities to people of every social and economic backgrounds that are willing to commit themselves to the hard work involved in obtaining a Bachelor of Arts Degree, information technology has changed rapidly. The Open University used correspondence via the post office, television, radio, face-to-face tutorials and computers for administration and testing. Today, advances in information technology have automated many of the delivery processes of 1971, and made the delivery of computer-based education more efficient. Just imagine that today you can have a face-to-face instruction from some one across the hall or around the world on a PC (equipped with a telephone, video camera and the right communication channel, and appropriate software) to your home.

At the local level, say in a small school or college, databases and multimedia electronic encyclopedias are available for use on a Local Area Network (LAN). A multimedia electronic encyclopedia on a local area network can allow many students in the same classroom or in different classrooms in the same building to access the same information simultaneously. This type of CD-ROM courseware often allows students to interact, and can even teach students how to express the meaning of a passage or, how to paraphrase the passage.

With changes in Wide Area Network (WAN) technology and WAN services, computers can deliver and distribute knowledge and quality education to small colleges or departments that were not possible before. Take a small college or department that wants to offer a quality curriculum and teach such subjects as calculus, logics, astrophysics, botany or zoology. According to present practices, such a college or department will not be able to establish any of these courses, if it does not have twenty students registered for each of these courses. With the capability of information technology, many colleges can connect to a network and participate jointly, thus, combining the number of students in each college or department to reach the required class size. The implication here is, with computers and information technology, a small college or department can now offer a curriculum with quality and high academic standing that hitherto was not allowed.

Wide Area Network

The network that provides the services of public and private packet-switching, high-speed lines, radio, cables, satellites or national telephone facility is called a Wide Area Network (WAN). A PC or LAN may be connected from a remote site to some computer facility hundreds or thousands of miles away using one or many channels of communication in a wide area network.

Rapid technological changes in PC hardware and peripherals, software design, and new services offered by carriers or WAN providers like Pacific Bell, Sprint, MCI and others threaten to reshape current network organizations. These changes will put more capability into the hands of people who can now get knowledge and educational instructions directly at their homes. They also can have a dialogue with tutors, other students, and even see their faces while sharing notes. This is possible through an Enterprise Network for remote and even mobile users. *Figure 6-2* shows a Block Diagram of an Enterprise Network for Remote and Mobile Users.

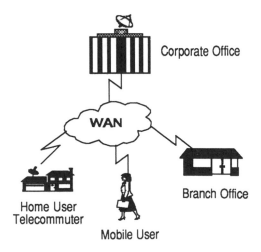

Figure 6-2. A Block Diagram of an Enterprise Network for Remote and Mobile Users

Bringing Education to the Learner at Home

Education and knowledge through remote access are of particular interest to people that have suffered physical injury or disability and are not able to fight their way through the commuter traffic and/or the growing costs, limitations, and parking problems that bedevil modern university and college campuses. Also, full-time workers, single parents, women on maternity leave, and people at outlying areas where seasonal weather can make traveling to a campus impassable, are all prime candidates for this type of education. Besides, there is a growing interest in flexibility of office hours and educational arrangements.

Improvement in the educational delivery system will provide an alternative to the conventional colleges and universities which require students to attend classes on a particular campus at a particular time. It also will provide flexible educational arrangements and save traveling time, parking hassles, parking fees and fines, classroom space, and eliminate the need to build more prestigious centers and hence, reduce overhead.

This upsurge of interest of learning by remote access also is driven by technology and competitiveness of the telecommunication carriers. Let us take a brief look at some technological developments leading to the possibility of bringing education to the learner at home by remote access.

Faster Personal Computers and Increased Bandwidth

Today's PCs have i80486 and Pentium-based microprocessors with speeds from 66 to 100 megahertz (MHz). MODEMs with 14.4 Kilobits per second are the norm although 28.8 kbps is now available. Also, one of those PCs can have an ISDN (Integrated Services Digital Network) Adapter with a ST or a NTI device that gives a PC the capability of transmitting up to 128 kbps - about nine times faster than any 14.4 kbps MODEM.

ISDN

The ISDN connectivity gives the PC sufficient bandwidth for transmitting video, audio, and data. This is useful when using graphic intensive programs or working with high volumes of data. Its response time far exceeds that of a MODEM and you can even experience personal conferencing in real-time with another PC using the right programs and peripherals.

Software

Many software products relating to remote access for PCs require 4 to 8 Megabytes (MB) of Random Access Memory (RAM) and 7 or 8 MB of hard disk space. Besides, there may be other communication software to consider. A high-end PC can have more secondary memory than some minicomputers a decade ago.

WAN Services

The telecommunication companies such as Pacific Bell and Sprint are offering new Wide Area Network (WAN) Services and lowering their charges on other services. For example, Pacific Bell offers dedicated digital services with physical connection between sites, Switched Digital Service Integrated systems (SDSI) with physical connection established on demand, faster packet services with single access to multiple destinations with x.25 packet service, Frame Relay, and other services. Sprint offers nationwide WAN service including Frame Relay, TCP/IP, Packet Switched data including x.25, dedicated data (private lines), switched data, Integrated Services, Digital Network (ISDN), switched voice and other services, such as router services.

With these developments, perhaps it is time to review the merits of attending certain conventional colleges and universities that are pricing themselves out of the market, even while engaging in mass production, as compared with more flexible alternatives.

Questions for Discussion and Review

1. What is Education? Distinguish between computers in Education and the services that computers can provide to an educational institution.

2. Explain the difference between administrative computing and instructional computing. Give examples.

3. What are the advantages of Computer Assisted (Aided) Instruction (CAI) and a Computer-based Education Laboratory over the traditional lecture technique of teaching?

4. Discuss the impact of computers on *pedagogy*.

5. Outline four obstacles to the effective use of computers as an instructional aid to teaching in higher education.

6. How can a computer system help students who lack basic skills in remedial education?

7. Explain how computers and information technology can improve the delivery of knowledge beyond the campus walls.

8. Explain the terms, LAN and WAN.

9. Some universities support Education Networks that provide "distance education" and deliver courses and academic programs to students off campus. Explain how this service can help a small college or university to offer a balanced curriculum.

10. With the availability of ISDN, *Internet*, and personal conferencing to individuals with PCs, an education network can be a viable alternative to conventional colleges and universities for delivering certain courses and program. Discuss.

Chapter 7 | Computer Simulation and Case Study as Alternative Teaching Methods

In engineering, physics, management science, medicine, and in the training of certain professionals, computer simulation and case study have been gaining ground as alternative teaching methods. This is in contrast with the traditional lecture where the instructor or professor lectures to students who listen, absorb, memorize, and perhaps do a *critique* of a hypothesis or theory.

Simulation and case study use scientific methods, and *purposeful* thinking to solve complex problems. A complex problem involves perception, organized thought, and an interdisciplinary approach to a problem whose solution path is not algorithmic or deterministic. This approach is suitable for the adult student, the senior, the graduate student or the professional who has been exposed to basic engineering concepts, or management science concepts or has a knowledge-base of the appropriate field of discipline related to the problem at hand. With such a prerequisite, the student can enrich and fortify his knowledge with a team approach to the solution process of a complex problem.

Scientific Methods

In this discussion on *scientific methods*, two types of structures are described. The first type involves observing the facts and setting up some hypotheses as the premises then using a deductive system to lead to the conclusion. The second type of structure is a systematic procedure that is conveyed in quantitative expressions and derived from analytical thought.

The first type of structure is a deductive system in which observable consequences logically follow from the conjunction of observed facts with a set of hypotheses as the premises where all the other hypotheses logically follow. The normal way to represent a deductive system is to write the sentences, formula, or other symbolic expressions that express the propositions in order so the spatial relationship of the sentences corresponds to the logical relationship between the propositions of the system. The deductions and conclusions are then verified along the line by its correspondence with facts. This type of scientific method is illustrated in later Chapters.

The second type of structure is made up of a series of processes or steps necessary for scientific investigation, generally taken to include rules for concept formation, conduct of observations and experiments, and validation of hypotheses by observations or experiments. This systematic procedure is conveyed in quantitative expressions and derived from analytical thought.

Let us look at the second type of structure more closely. This structure outlines a series of processes or steps for a scientific investigation. The steps are as follows:

1. Make observations of the real system. These stimulate ideas about the process being observed.
2. Formulate a hypothesis that attempts to explain clearly and formally the observations of the system.
3. Make predictions of the behavior of the system on the basis of the hypothesis by using mathematical or statistical estimation or logical deductions.
4. Devise and perform an experiment to *test* the validity of the hypothesis or model.
5. On the basis of the experiment, which provides new observations, the hypothesis is *either accepted or rejected.*
6. If the hypothesis is rejected, a new hypothesis may be formed, then tested in turn.

Although it is important to understand these two methods of scientific investigation, we must indicate that often in real-life decision taking, it is not always possible to follow all the steps outlined above. When this arises, some form of *simulation* may be a satisfactory substitute. For example, where it was impossible to observe the real system, as in space technology, simulation was the only technique to test what might happen. Also, sometimes it could be prohibitively expensive if not impossible to obtain all the data. Thus, *simulation* is an important method for studying real-life decision taking, and for training executives, engineers, aircraft pilots and other professionals in decision-making.

Elements of Simulation

Without using lots of symbols and mathematical jargon, the basic approach to a simulation model is to obtain a logical understanding of the basic elements of the model. A *simulation* model consists of four elements: components, variables, parameters, and functional relationships.

The *components*, for example, of the model of a college could be the departments.

The *variables are* used to relate one component to another. There are *exogenous variables, status variables and endogenous variables.*

The *parameters* are estimated values derived by statistical inference for the operating characteristics, for example, means and standard deviations of known probability distribution.

The *functional relationships* describe the interaction of the variables and components. There are two types of functional relationships: (a) *identities*, definition statements such as:

Total Profit = Total Revenue − Total Costs

and, (b) *operating characteristics*, which are the various probability distributions used in the model. Other methods like the *Monte Carlo Techniques* are used for problems having a stochastic/probabilistic base and the use of random sampling techniques to achieve the required accuracy and to evaluate different decision strategies.

Some Advantages of Simulation

With simulation, executives or students can learn about different possibilities and how to arrive at the best decision without making direct experimentation, which can be costly, time consuming, and even disruptive. For example, in planning the layout and design of a factory and office occupancy, students can build a model of the factory and the office; templates to represent the items of machinery, and even use different color schemes to select the best color of the carpet for the office. Students can rearrange the different items of machinery in a factory in the model on a computer and observe the results. The process may be repeated, and the students can make further rearrangements until all logical possibilities have been exhausted. Eventually, one such arrangement is judged best. The same procedure is applied to the color of the carpet and the office arrangement.

A computer simulation of the layout of the factory and office is preferable to having large items of machinery delivered then move them around to make different arrangements. In this example, the method of direct observation of the real items would be time consuming, disruptive and costly, particularly when power, cabling and installations have to be scheduled in advance. Therefore, computer simulation using a model to represent the items of machinery in a factory or colors of carpet in the design of an office provides not only the best and least costly decision, but a useful learning experience for the decision-maker.

Indirect Experimentation

Indirect experimentation using computer simulation is an invaluable learning experience. Take the design of a modern aircraft, the procedure is to evaluate several design proposals and configurations by building a model of each configuration then test each model in a wind tunnel. This procedure gives designers information and knowledge about which design and configurations are good, safe and economical before constructing a full-scale prototype, which has to be flight tested under real conditions. Although building a full-scale prototype is an essential step, direct experimentation without a computer simulation would be very costly, if not dangerous.

The Case Study Method

The case study method has been used for many years in prominent business schools, schools of engineering and Departments of Management Science. The case study method is particular effective in transforming those students (whose intellectual developments in their college years have made them habitual receivers) from receivers to constructive thinkers. This goal is very important for honor students or students entering graduate schools of business, engineering or medicine. For example, in an established graduate School of Business Administration, a case study is a managerial problem that actually has been faced by business executives in some organization with partial facts, beliefs, and opinions upon which executive decisions depend. Students under this method are given specific facts, opinions, and some data. The information and data presented could be inadequate whereby the student must seek to acquire the necessary information, make reasonable assumptions out of which decisions have to be made.

The case study method is an excellent *off-the-job* training vehicle, if carried out in a simulated job situation similar to or identical with the real job environment. It provides learning by constructive thinking and doing.

Students must assess and analyze a problem situation; develop solutions to the problem presented; evaluate his or her position as well as the positions of fellow students from different disciplines; and cooperate with fellow students and the instructor to provide the best solution. The case study method dramatizes the situation to resemble real-life decision-making in certain circumstances and under certain conditions. This allows role-playing and students' participation. This also teaches the student how to give and receive different ideas and have confidence so that upon graduation they have a chance of fulfilling their cherished hope of finding a position of authority.

The case study method also let students realize that the best solution to a complex problem may require an *interdisciplinary* approach. An *interdisciplinary* approach involves persons trained in different fields of disciplines with different concepts, methods, data, tools and terms organized into a common effort to solve a common problem with continuous intercommunication among the participants from different disciplines. The total learning experience gained from a well-prepared case study, can give students an insight into real-world decision-making that they will cherish after graduation. The following is an abstract from the Tennek Electronic Company's case study, which gives us some ideas of the various types of information required for a complex problem.

Tennek Electronic Company - A Case Study

Problem and Beliefs. Let us consider the case of Tennek Electronic Company. This company has a *patent* for a cooling device that can be attached easily inside the casing of television sets, monitors, computers and specific electronic products. The product designer is very excited about this device and wants Tennek Electronic Company to produce and sell the device. The designer believes that his invention is a breakthrough and wants management to start production as soon as possible.

If there is unlimited sources of money, materials, labor, and capital, the President of Tennek Electronic Company can say go ahead and acquire all the necessary factors of production and produce the cooling device, then go and sell it. But without some firm information from major buyers guaranteeing orders with a total expected value greater than the total cost of the project, such a decision is regarded as a high risk with great uncertainty.

Knowledge and the Need for Information

In a complex situation where there are high risks and a high degree of uncertainty, knowledge about logical decision-making processes can improve the efficiency of choice. Information about the problem also reduces the degree of uncertainty. Thus, knowledge and information are required to confirm or disprove beliefs. So, in the Tennek Electronic problem, a management information system framework is needed to solve this problem efficiently and rationally. Now, let us look at the types of information needed and their characteristics.

Greater Demands Than Available Resources. In a modern business enterprise, college, or university there are always limitations and constraints on the availability of resources. Against these constraints are demands to produce, distribute and sell to a certain number of customers at the best price, or in a college or university demands for services. Besides the mismatch between available resources and varying demands, there are certain dynamics in the environment that require rapid response, which may not be possible without the use of a computer. Under these conditions, management and its decision-makers may go through a strategy of risk aversion. They may construct a chart with a preference value that translates monetary consequence into utility values, which typically range from zero to one; or they may do a break-even analysis, which is a method of determining the level of activity at which total revenue will equal total costs.

Some Reasons for Logical Decision and Quantitative Techniques

Many important decisions are made intuitively. Judgement and experience tend to form the basis of many decisions, but a logical analysis using mathematical and quantitative techniques can provide information that will give management measurable advantages in appraising alternative courses of action. When managerial judgement is needed and where some mangers do not have an intimate enough knowledge of the different types of information needed before launching a new product, certain information must be provided and assimilated. Let us now take a brief look at the different types of information needed to make a rational decision. Also, let us consider the different concepts, methods, and approaches from the different fields of disciplines in solving this problem. The problem is whether to produce and sell a new cooling device that will draw off heat in television sets, monitors, computers and other electronic products.

Economic Theory and Sales Forecasting

How the management of Tennek Electronic Company will arrive at a decision to launch a new product or not, will depend to a large extent on their educational background, experience, and their information and knowledge about the industry. In some circumstances, the company may conduct a survey based on the elementary economic theory of the firm. The economist will go through the supply and demand theories. He or she will take the prices of other related firms as given, then make some self-justifying price configurations and come out with a conclusion whether there is a demand for the product or not. The management may want to do some statistical analysis, using *secular trends* with linear, weighted, exponential methods or *regression analysis* and an analysis of variance to forecast and project sales in the short and long term.

Market Research and Decision Logic

The management can then conduct a market-research survey, which can cost up to $50,000 to establish whether or not the product has the potential for success as shown on the type of report described above. If the market-research shows that the product does not have a potential for success, the company can cut its losses by selling all its rights in the product. On the other hand, if the survey shows that the product has potential, a test-marketing operation can be carried out in a carefully selected locality at a cost of say $100,000. Should the test-marketing result become favorable, a strategic launch of the product will follow.

Reorganization and New Skills Requirement

At the point where a decision is made to go ahead and prepare to launch a new product, some reorganization may have to take place. A cost and management accountant, and a system and production engineer may have to be hired. The management accountant should have professional knowledge and skill in the design, implementation, control and maintenance of the management information system. The cost and management accountant needs communication skills and considerable analytical ability to give relevant information and advice on a wide range of problems.

The cost and management accountant must have knowledge of costing principles, methods and techniques in the ascertainment of cost and the analysis of savings and comparing previous experience with standards. He must understand fully the nature of the company and the environment in which it operates. Also, he or she should regard the company as a system of parts interrelated and working together to achieve a common purpose. He or she must have the ability to coordinate the efforts of a team of managers to effect good budgetary control, and work with the production manager to obtain output at satisfactory quality and costs.

Responsibilities

Product design and development activities have to be carried out. These involve specifying what is to be produced, the preparation of drawings, specifications, formulas and other instructions to the production department.

The system engineer or production engineer is responsible for deciding and specifying how the work is to be done. The main activities include an investigation of the methods, designer's setting of tools and equipment, the measurement of work and establishment of standard times. Also, production planning, which involves deciding and issuing schedules for when work is to be done, and materials and stock records, preparation of long and short-term manufacturing programs, shop and machine loading and progress chasing is required.

The system engineer or production engineer's activities also include production control, which is concerned with recording the results and correcting deviations from programs and variations from standards. Depending upon the size of the company or its organization, purchasing function is an important part of the operation of the company. A knowledgeable person should be responsible for buying the materials required for production, and all other items and supplies not manufactured in the company's own plant. He or she has to find suppliers, negotiate prices and other conditions, and place official orders.

Closer Cooperation between Production and Marketing

Production should be integrated with the marketing and distribution activities. If the marketing strategy is to go for seasonal marketing, the production must be flexible to respond. Production programs must reflect marketing and distribution plans such as building up capacity of plant or sections of the works to meet changes in demand or emphasis in advertising.

Advertising Provides Information and Knowledge

Advertising is a method of providing potential buyers with knowledge of the identity of the product or the seller. It is clearly a powerful instrument for the elimination of ignorance compared with an oral discourse to communicate knowledge. Advertising is the search to identify the product and the seller. The identification of the seller is necessary because the identity of sellers changes, as there is a turnover of buyers over time. In the consumer market there are normally new buyers entering the market because of either immigration or people attaining financial maturity. In this situation, it is important to advertise to refresh the knowledge of infrequent buyers and to identify the product or seller to the new buyers.

Advertising also helps management to discover the best prices. Prices change with varying frequency in most markets. Unless a market is completely centralized, management cannot know all the prices, that various sellers quote at a given time. A seller or buyer who wishes to ascertain the most competitive or favorable price must go among sellers (or buyers) asking for prices. Knowledge of competitive prices gives management the necessary information for negotiating the asking prices of consumers and producer goods respectively.

Capital Budgeting

It may be necessary to acquire additional capital to produce the new cooling product. This may involve large sums of money and a decision of this type can influence the operation of the business in the future. This requires capital budgeting, which is concerned with investment decisions within the business. The capital budgeting problem arises from an attempt to allocate limited investment funds between competing claims to funds for potential investment projects to increase the company's earnings potential.

This may involve two separate but interrelated capital budgeting problems. The first is capital appraisal and acquisition, and the second is investment financing.

Capital Appraisal and Acquisition

The rationing of funds between competing projects requires the establishment of selection criteria. Rarely, is there only one equipment to choose from and a careful evaluation of alternatives is essential. For when we are considering a machinery or system to carry out specified tasks, there are frequently several new machines or systems will perform satisfactorily. But each machine or system might involve a different investment and different rate of return.

The clue to this dilemma is to *screen* the different machineries or proposals to see whether a proposal offers a satisfactory return or not. A minimum satisfactory rate of return must be determined and the physical life, the technological life, the product-market life, and the cost of the capital (proposal) should be factors in this determination. After this procedure and assuming that satisfactory proposals have now been short-listed, the next procedure is to rank the proposals in order of *preference*. Which of the short-list of proposals is the best? Which is the next best and so forth. Several financial methods are available for assisting management in the selection of a capital investment proposal.

When you take into consideration the physical life, the technological life, the product-market life, and the cost of the proposal, at least three simple financial methods can be used to assist management in their preference for one proposal over another. They are the *pay-back method, the return on investment method,* and the *present value method.*

Pay-back Method. This method attempts to determine the length of time (or number of years) in which the cash inflow or revenue from the proposal equals the total initial cash outlay. Thus, the number of years in which the investment is expected to pay for itself. For example, if the total cost of a proposal is $50,000, and the revenue expected from the proposal amounts to $10,000 in the first year, $20,000 in the second year and $20,000 in the third year then the pay-back period is three years. Some investors argue that this calculation should look at earnings after tax, thus net cash inflow. However, this argument requires other considerations, which are discussed in another volume covering financial systems.

Return on Investment Method. This method considers the rate of return to be obtained from the investment. The rate of return is expressed as a percentage of the investment. So, when comparing alternative proposals, the investment that shows the highest rate of return is normally selected. There are different variations of this calculation. Some investors like to take the percentage of the average amount of the investment, so that the "average" is to divide the total investment by two.

A way to understand this method is to consider a bank that lends Tennek Electronic Company $50,000 and receives an interest payment of $4,000 at the end of each year for five years with the loan being repaid at the end of the fifth year. The bank will earn a return of 8% on its investment of $50,000.

The Present Value Method. A business person will not invest $100 *now* for one year unless he or she will get back more than the $100 next year. That is, the business person expects to earn a return on the investment he or she makes. Put another way, if a person is given the choice of having $100 *now* or in one year's time, it is very likely that person will elect to have the $100 *now*. On the other had, if he or she was offered $100 *now*, but $110 in a year's time, then he or she may consider waiting for one year and get $110. Therefore, he or she is foregoing $100 *now* to earn 10% more one year later. Since the business person expects to earn 10% on the $100 in one year, a $100 at the end of a year has a *present value* today of only $90.91. And, the expectation of receiving $100 in *two* years from today has a present value of $82.64. A formula for calculating present values is as follows:

For payment of $1 to be received *n* years, at any rate of return (*i*).

$$\frac{1}{(1+i)^n}$$

But you may not have to use this formula if you have a present value table. A present value table is an orderly arrangement containing number of years from this year hence with corresponding present values of $1 at a discounted rate of return based on a certain percent.

Investment Financing

After going through all the various alternatives, management must decide how they will finance the proposed project. Management must decide whether they will provide funds through retained profits and savings or from external sources. Internal finance has the advantage of being free from the whims of the money market. Also, it makes the company less vulnerable to the behavior of the central bank, which uses the prime rate of interest as a monetary policy to control the economy. A disadvantage of internal financing is that capital expenditure may impede long-term growth and other worthwhile projects may be held back for lack of funds. There also is the possibility that management may have to cut dividends, and shareholders may protest.

External financing is not always readily available, for the supply of capital is affected by conditions in the money market. The price of capital also fluctuates and can be so high as to disqualify otherwise useful or productive projects.

Besides these financial considerations, management may want to explore the option to lease or buy the equipment in the proposal. A *lease* is a contractual agreement between a *lessor* and *lessee* that conveys to the lessee the right to use specific property (real or personal) owned by the lessor, for a specific period in return for stipulated, and generally periodic cash payments. Leasing has several advantages. Leasing permits 100% of financing versus 75% to 90% under purchasing, thus conserving cash and working capital. Leasing also permits write-off of the full cost of the asset (including the residual value) and provides additional tax advantages through accelerations of deductions.

Conclusion

An explanation of the types of decisions, the need for interaction between different departments, the role of information and knowledge, and the need for proper financial analysis is worthwhile, particular in an age of information technology and competition. Simulation and information technology can lead to efficiency, profitability and the company's ability to adapt to changes in the environment.

Simulation, case studies and games provide very effective teaching/learning situations. They are not limited to business decisions They are being used in engineering, medicine, town and regional planning, and as a teaching vehicle in training pilots of new aircrafts. Simulation is particularly useful in teaching subjects where alternative courses of action have to be considered, and real-life decisions taken.

Questions for Discussion and Review

1. What is simulation? Describe briefly the elements of a simulation model.

2. Explain how computer simulation can be used successfully as an alternative teaching method. Give at least two examples.

3. Why is computer simulation a desired method for training aircraft pilots, and astronauts?

4. What is a Case Study? Explain how the use of the case study method in teaching certain subjects can prove helpful for students a learning experience in contrast with the traditional approach of teaching.

5. The case study method is being used in many graduate business schools. What educational values can be gained from a case study?

6. Some complex problems require an *interdisciplinary* approach to problem solving. Discuss, and illustrate your answer with some examples.

Chapter 8

Knowledge, Logic and the Development of Intelligent Computer Systems

Knowledge and logic are closely related with the development of knowledge based systems, a term synonymous with "expert systems." An expert system is a computer-based system containing knowledge about objects, events, situations and courses of action to emulate the reasoning processes of a human expert in a particular field of knowledge or domain. However, it is essential to have an understanding of modern symbolic logic to fully appreciate the development of an expert system.

The role of knowledge as a social value and a product has occupied the interests of philosophers, educators and economists throughout the world for centuries, long before the computer was invented. Unlike the so called "advanced societies," which place emphasis on skyscrapers and the abundance of consumer-durable goods, and where people adore lots of money and material possessions, earlier generations have always respected knowledgeable people. Knowledgeable people, were the Swamis, (the religious Hindu teachers), the masters of the Buddhist monasteries, the rabbis, clergymen, scholars, philosophers, and teachers. People came to them for advice. These knowledgeable people enumerated reasons for their problems and suggested solutions based on rule of thumb methods, and the people in their community were grateful for their advice.

Schools, universities, laboratories, and corporations also transmit and generate knowledge. Some of the knowledge transmitted is new knowledge produced by faculty, researchers, and scientists through research and scholarship. Some of the new research is useful, and a very small part of it can be very important, in that it has the potential to offer a cure or improve the method of treatment for a serious disease or to improve the production of goods and services.

Another producer of new knowledge is the computer. Most of the new knowledge generated from faculty, researchers and scientists is due in part to the computer. However, in this Chapter, emphasis is placed on knowledge generated by the computer.

Knowledge

The word *knowledge* has two meanings:

1. The possession of a fact or a state of knowing with clarity or certainty. For example, malaria is an infectious disease characterized by chills, fever, and sweating; or saline is a solution containing (sodium chloride) salt; or, the print head of a 24-pin dot matrix printer consists of a stack of 24 pins, which print each character as a group or matrix of dots on impact.

2. The possession of a skill or expertise, or an understanding gained through study, training and experience. For example, Ken has knowledge of *Kendo* (the art of Japanese swordsmanship). Isabel is an expert of tropical diseases. Tina has received training in printer technology, and has experience in diagnosing and repairing printers.

With the first meaning, we can say that knowledge is made up of facts which are derived from information that has been selected, interpreted, transformed and known to have happened or to be true. We can call this type of knowledge *declarative knowledge*. We can use a database program to store in a computer, facts about malaria and its attributes, or about saline, or dot matrix printers, or about any domain of knowledge. Users of such a database can retrieve information and factual knowledge about a domain, but have to draw their own conclusion. The database program does not draw conclusions.

The second meaning signifies knowledge as having a skill, or expertise in a domain of knowledge. It implies training, experience, abilities in deciding courses of action, and knowing the causes.

An expert of tropical diseases can integrate the properties of the *declarative knowledge* with procedures, rules and action, on the domain of knowledge, called malaria. This, of course, would apply to a different expert in a different domain of knowledge. Computer scientists call this type of procedure or rule, *heuristic.* I will explain this term later in this Chapter.

Logic

Logic was introduced by the ancient Greeks, long before computers were invented. But George Boole (1815-64), Augustus de Morgan (1806-71) W.S. Jevons (1835-82), C.S. Pierce (1839-1914), Bertrand Russell and A.N. Whitehead in *Principia Mathematica,* and others have made important logical discoveries. These discoveries led to a reform of classical logic into, what we call today, modern logic or symbolic logic.

Logic is the study of deductions, and the principles of reasoning. It is also concerned with knowledge, truths, judgements, statements (or propositions), the rules of thinking and the forms of thought. Logic also is important because it gives us a way of valid reasoning as distinguished from invalid or irrational arguments or unsubstantial beliefs. Computer scientists including cyberneticians and artificial intelligence specialists use logic to represent knowledge, define relationships and rules of inference to draw conclusions. Let us take a brief look at some parts of modern symbolic logic to get an appreciation of the development of a knowledge based system (expert system).

Propositions

Let us use propositions as the starting point for our appreciation of modern symbolic logic. A proposition is a sentence in which the subject is affirmed or denied by the predicate and can or is shown to be true or false. The elements and terms of a proposition may be looked at from linguistic rules or from the calculus of propositions, also known as propositional calculus, which is a branch of logic.

To make a point about logic and linguistics, let us take the sentence or statement, "Doris is Dad's sister." In English, sentences and statements are generally capable of being split into subject and predicate. The subject represents a "term," which is the name of some class of objects and a predicate term that says something about the subject and copulas. Copulas are verbs and connecting words, clauses and relational connectives, such as, and, or, equal, not greater than, less than, and so on. In the sentence "Doris is Dad's sister," I am saying something about a relationship between two people or between two classes of objects. Similarly, the relationship between these two people could be represented by some letter such as R and the two people by any two letters such as x and y.

Syllogism

One of the principal logical forms which has been systematically investigated over centuries by eminent philosophers and mathematicians, is the *syllogism*. The *syllogism* is a form of argument where a direct inference is made from two propositions to a third. An *inference* is a process of reasoning consisting of forming conclusions from premises. The first two propositions consist of a major premise and a minor premise, like axioms, but the third proposition, which is the conclusion is like a theorem. Let us look at the following example:

(1) All basketball players are energetic (*major premise*).
Michael Jordan is a basketball player (*minor premise*).
Therefore, Michael Jordan is energetic (*Conclusion*).

The first two propositions are rather like axioms, but the third proposition, which is the conclusion, is rather like a theorem. This is a valid argument by virtue of its relationships. However, we can express this form of argument in this way:

(2) All B's are E's.
J is a B
Therefore, J is E.

Now consider the next example:

(3) If all basketball players are energetic
and Michael Jordan is a basketball player,
then Michael Jordan is energetic.

The logical structure or form of argument also can be expressed as:

(4) If *a* and *b,* then *c.*

Let us look at some more examples:

(5) Shamu is a whale.
If Shamu is a whale, then he is a mammal.
Shamu is a mammal.

(6) Shamu is a whale.
All whales are bigger than all dolphins.
Shamu is bigger than all dolphins.

(7) Either Charles is dishonest or some accountants are careless

(8) Exmoor Pony exists

(9) Stallion exists

Example (5) begins with the following two statements:

Shamu is a whale.
If Shamu is a whale, then he is a mammal.

If shamu is a whale, then he is a mammal. If we assume that both statements are true, then the inference rule of propositional calculus tells us that the following statement also must be true.

Shamu is a mammal.

Predicate Calculus

Predicate calculus is based on propositional calculus and uses its methods and its notation to form a new type of logical structure with which it has to deal. Predicate calculus deals not only with relations between propositions as a whole, or truth-functional analysis, but adds the capability of specifying relationships between the subject and the predicate and making generalizations. As usual, symbols are used to represent the subject and predicate of a proposition and the *existential* or universal quantified is used to denote whether the proposition is universal or particular in its application.

Example (6) begins with the following two statements:

Shamu is a whale.
All whales are bigger than all dolphins.

Notice the second statement includes the following generalization: "All whales" and "All dolphins" and the relationship, "are bigger than." If these two statements are true, then the rules of predicate calculus will let you make the following conclusion:

Shamu is bigger than all dolphins.

Example (6) is called a compound proposition, which is composed of any two simple propositions. The propositional formula "p v q" allows you to unite these two simple propositions by the word "or" taken in its inclusive sense.

Examples (8) and (9) deal with the particular quantifier. The propositions:

(8) Exmoors exist
(9) Stallions exist

are not singular propositions because they contain no proper names. The word "exist" is not a proper description. The assertion that Exmoors exist does not tell you what Exmoors are. How then, are such propositions to be analyzed? First, let us interpret these two propositions:

8.1 There is something, which is an exmoor.
9.1 There is something, which is a stallion.

These two sentences express the same proposition of the first two. Now, if we split (8.1) and (9.1) each into two parts, we note:

8.2 (There is something) (which is an exmoor).
9.2 (There is something) (which is a stallion).

In using elementary algebra, you can use the letters "x," "y," and "z" for the written words "something" and "which." Thus, 8.3 and 9.3 become:

8.3 (There is an x) (x is an exmoor).
9.3 (There is an x) (x is a stallion).

You can use arbitrary letters like "f" and "g" as predicate symbols. So that "f" for "is an exmoor" in 8.3 and "g" for a stallion in 9.3

8.4 (There is an x) (fx)
9.4 (There is an x) (gx)

First Order Predicate Calculus

By adding *function* and other analytical and annotated concepts to predicate calculus, we can formulate descriptions of individual objects, relevant problem-oriented information, and formulate resultant concept descriptions. This form of logic expression is called *first-order predicate calculus.*

This notion of using *first-order* logic on computer-based intelligent systems can be traced back to the early period of *Artificial Intelligence* (AI) research. Newell, A. and Simon, H.A. "The Logic Theory Machine," McCarthy, J., "First Order Theories of Individual Concepts and Propositions," and others used *first-order predicate calculus* for knowledge representation and problem-solving systems.

A *function* is a construct or mapping f from a set of X to a set of Y, denoted by $f: X \rightarrow Y$, associated with each element of x of X a single element y of Y, denoted by $f(x)$. A *function* also is a logical construct that indicates a relationship of belonging to, and it brings back or returns a value. For example, by adding a *belongs-to* or *is-owned-by* function to Shamu will return Sea World, a list representing that knowledge may look like either of these.

(*BELONGS-TO* (SHAMU SEA WORLD))
(*IS-OWNED-BY* (SHAMU SEA WORLD))

By using *first-order predicate calculus*, you can create a knowledge-based program of which you can ask "who Shamu belongs-to?" or "Who owns Shamu?" It will return a value of Sea World. Thus, it will tell you that Shamu belongs to Sea World.

Fuzzy Set

In the real world there are many situations and events that are fuzzy and not sharply defined. Probability theory may be used to measure the strength of some belief expressed as a ratio or percentage of the likelihood of a specific event occurring. It also can tell you if there are two events. E_1 and E_2, the probability that E_2 occurs given that E_1 has occurred. However, probability theory cannot handle concepts that are relative and approximate. So, *fuzzy set* and *fuzzy Algorithm* was proposed by Zadeh (1973).

Zadeh proposed a *fuzzy set algorithm* to handle relative and approximate descriptions such as "the flowers are beautiful," "the girl resembles her mother," "the man is tall," "the camera is expensive," "the temperature is moderate" and so on. In *fuzzy* set theory, each object is characterized by a membership function that assigns a grade of membership varying between zero and one. The *fuzzy* set algorithm also is useful in classifying real-world objects of classes that do not possess sharply defined boundaries as in the usual mathematical sense.

Graphs and Semantic Network

In the fields of information processing systems, mathematics, and other domains, graphs and networks provide a more convenient representation of input, events, and concept descriptions of objects and their parts than logical expressions. The arrangement of nodes and connecting branches can be used to define complex interrelationships to represent facts as nodes and their relationships to other facts as the links or arcs. When used in this manner, it is called a *semantic network* or a *semantic net*.

Let us draw a simple *semantic network* to depict some facts and their relationships to other facts. See *Figure 8-1*.

A semantic network can simplify the process of deduction. For example, a visual look at the semantic network in Figure 8-1 will reveal that Shamu is a mammal and is bigger than a dolphin, though there is no direct connection between the Shamu Node and the Mammal Node and Dolphin Node. In English, one can reason in the following manner, "A whale is a mammal and is bigger than a dolphin"; "Shamu is whale, therefore, Shamu is a mammal and is bigger than a dolphin." An artificial Intelligence program that uses this semantic network for knowledge representation also will be able to answer such questions as, "Is Shamu bigger than a dolphin?" "Is a dolphin a mammal?" and, "who owns Shamu?"

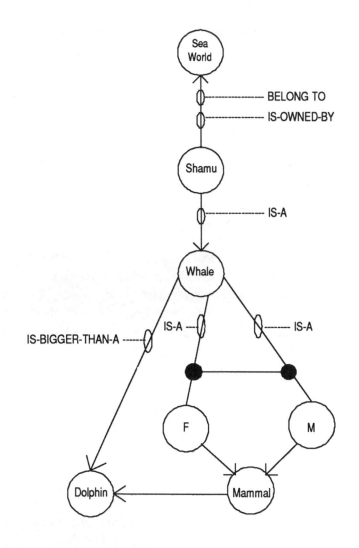

Figure 8-1. A Simple Semantic Network

Production System

When designing a knowledge-based system/expert system, which recommends a course of action, it is more efficient to use a *productive system* that contains not only facts about objects, but also includes knowledge of what to do with those facts. A *production system* uses *production rules* to represent *procedural* knowledge about the action to take in a specific situation. Put simply, a production rule is a form of "IF-THEN" or "Condition-action" statement or pair (C → A), where C is a set of conditions and A is a sequence of actions. If all the conditions in the production rule are satisfied, the sequence of actions is executed. In the real world, production rules are formal representations of *heuristic*.

Heuristic comes from human experience acquired from books, learning, experience after performing certain tasks repeatedly and successfully and from practitioners' knowledge. This repository of a working rule of thumb approach provides a plausible inference or procedure for solving problems, where precise knowledge is lacking. For example, the following could be stated as a production rule:

Example (10)

PREMISE[1]: If the weather is cold, and you are having trouble starting your car, starter cannot crank engine.

ACTION[1] : Then check battery.

PREMISE[2] : If battery voltage test shows a low reading.

ACTION[2] : Do "jump-start," else replace bad battery.

Notice there are two basic clauses to each production rule: the *conditional* clause or *left-hand side* of a production rule, which begins with IF and specifies the condition or situation that must exist. The *action* clause, or the *right-hand* side, of a production rule, begins with THEN and specifies the action to take if the condition is satisfied.

Production rules are widely used as knowledge representation in knowledge-based, learning systems and problem-solving systems. *Rule-based systems* have become popular, since Bruce Buchanan and Edward Shortliffe developed MYCIN in the early 1970s, as part of the Heuristic Programming Project at Stanford University. MYCIN is an expert system that helps diagnose bacteriological blood infection.

Davis R., and Lenat. R., in "Knowledge-Based Systems in Artificial Intelligence" (1982) also found production rules useful in knowledge representation. They believed that the general task of deduction "fits quite well into situation/action character statements," and a transformation is necessary between "knowledge as expressed by the expert and its final encoding inside the system."

As you can see, the production system greatly helps the process of transferring knowledge from an expert in a particular field of knowledge to a computer. Because of their simplicity and general use, production rules are widely used as knowledge representation for knowledge-based systems or expert systems. In the next Chapter, we will explain the steps in developing an expert system, and describe the characteristics of an Intelligent Computer System that can amplify human intelligence.

Questions for Discussion and Review

1. What is the importance of formal logic in higher education?

2. Explain three characteristics of symbolic logic.

3. What are the reasons for using first-order calculus in the development of an intelligent computer system?

4. What are semantic networks? Give two examples, and state the advantages of a semantic network over text or mathematical expressions.

5. What are production rules? How are production rules related to rule-based systems? Give examples.

6. Before the turn of the twentieth century, knowledgeable people were philosophers, religious leaders, teachers, and experts in a trade, a profession, art or business. These knowledgeable people often used a *heuristic* approach to solve problems. What is a *heuristic* approach? Give examples.

Chapter 9

The Structure of an Expert System

Knowledge is an essential element or a necessary condition of an expert system. Knowledge acquisition (including expertise acquisition) is an important condition of learning. Knowledge of how an expert solves problems is likely to lead to developments in other related fields, such as intelligent computer-assisted instructions, and computer-based tutoring systems. Such developments also can lead to more effective educational tools.

The economic value of knowledge and expert system can be considerable, particular in areas where human experts are scarce or not available. In such situations, an artificial system that can replicate and distribute expert knowledge and give therapy or advice on a particular disorder or problem would be of tremendous economic and social value to a professional, institution, or a company where experts are not available or affordable.

Expert systems attempt to capture expertise and knowledge about a particular domain from a human expert and incorporate the knowledge and problem-solving strategies in a computer. This is done with the aid of a *knowledge engineer* (an AI specialist), system engineers, programmers, models, procedures and development tools. The principal parts or subsystems that make up an expert system are: knowledge component, inference system, meta-rules/utility control program, and the user interface.

There are different types of expert systems. The three main types are: *rule-based* systems, *frame-based* systems, and *model-based* systems. In this Chapter, we will look at *rule-based* systems. A diagram describing the principal parts and functions of an expert system is presented in *Figure 9-1*.

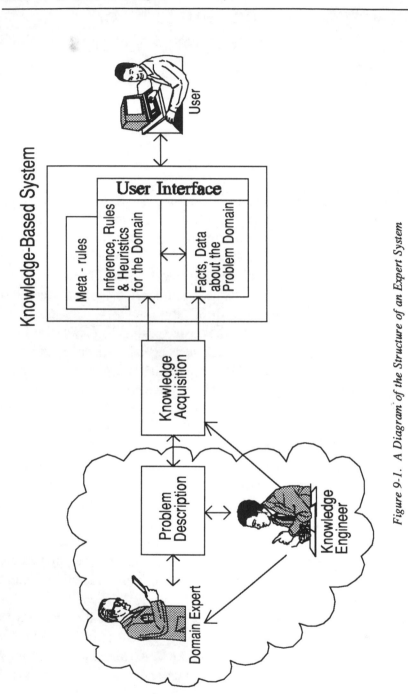

Figure 9-1. A Diagram of the Structure of an Expert System

Human Expert

The expert is a human expert who is specialized in a real-world problem task. The expert knows how to solve certain problems, and can explain what he/she does, and determine the reliability of his conclusion. This type of person is called a *domain expert*, and works closely with the knowledge engineer, (an AI specialist) in developing the expert system.

Knowledge Engineer

The knowledge engineer is an AI specialist who knows how to represent knowledge in a computer. Also, the person must have the following characteristics:

- Sound knowledge of the different types of knowledge representation.
- The ability to think logically, symbolically and abstractly.
- The person can work well with experts and other people as a team.
- Knowledge of LISP, PROLOG and other programming languages. Also, the person must have a knowledge of natural language programming.
- Knowledge of data structure.
- Good knowledge of the capability of computer hardware, firmware, and peripherals.
- Knowledge of interviewing techniques.

Knowledge Representation

Knowledge is stored in the brain of the human expert, and the knowledge engineer needs to understand the various types of knowledge representation to be able to capture it in the knowledge-base and inference system. There are many types of knowledge representations. They include decision trees, production rules, logical and relational expressions, network (neural nets), formal grammars, schema, and multiple representations. We have already discussed some types of knowledge representations in Chapter 8. But with advances in information technology, AI researchers must consider other types of knowledge representation including audio/visual representations.

Knowledge-based Systems (Expert System)

The knowledge-based system depicted in *Figure 9-1* has four principal parts: the *knowledge component* (facts and data about the domain), an *inference system* (including rules and heuristics), *meta-rules/ utility control program*, and a *user interface*. Let me describe them briefly in the following sections.

Knowledge Component

The knowledge component consists of facts, objects, and that which is known about the domain. This component is an essential part of the *knowledge base*. It consists of a collection of interrelated facts, events and situations of domain-specific knowledge stored as a base for use by the expert system program. This collection may be represented as *(objects)* or concepts about which information is stored, *(attributes)* or facts that characterize the object, and *(values)*. A *value* is the actual data or information contained in each *data element*. The values taken by the data elements can be quantitative, qualitative, or descriptive, depending on how the data elements are described at the object level. This collection of actual knowledge is similar to a database program. It also is called *declarative knowledge*.

Inference System

The inference system, often called *inference engine,* is the other essential component that is used with the knowledge component to make up the knowledge base of the expert system. It contains inference procedures, production rules and heuristics in the form of a suite of programs.

The inference system *(inference engine)* selects the rules to be used to determine the solution. It acts upon and draws conclusions by reasoning about the facts, events and situations in its domain. It is like an interpreter (with information about courses of actions) that uses the knowledge component to solve a problem or choose a course of action. Knowledge gained in this manner is called *procedural knowledge.*

Meta-Rules Utility Control Program

This is an intelligent program that prescribes the conditions, sequence and manner in which a given set of rules should be applied, rather like rules about the rules of the expert system. The meta-rules program also maintains utility information about the way the current representation is performing, and can generate new knowledge automatically.

Not all expert systems have this program. So, let us look at the reason for meta-rules utility control program. Artificial Intelligence (AI) researchers or expert system developers usually experience two trends after the acceptance of a prototype of a domain specific knowledge-base system. The first trend is a desire to insert more facts, events and situations of the domain specific knowledge in the computer.

The second trend is to concentrate on problems taken from real world conditions and use more *heuristics* to solve these problems. Both trends will result in an accumulation of a larger base of knowledge and rule interpreting. Maintaining a large base of knowledge and production rules can be cumbersome and time consuming. So, an intelligent control, or a meta-level program that manages the rules and uses inferences from them to generate new knowledge automatically is employed to improve the system capability.

This meta-level program should evaluate how well the current representations are performing. It should specify conditions under which certain rules should be followed instead of others. It should enable the knowledge-based system to respond to situations in which the language for describing a heuristic is insufficient. It should decide which heuristic *search techniques* are to be used. It should be able to discover new rules and new heuristics from the existing production system. It also should be able to modify existing rules and heuristics and learn how to detect and rectify inconsistencies and simplify production rules where necessary. Knowledge generated in this manner is known as *meta-level knowledge*.

User Interface

The user interface is an import part of an expert system. It involves the hardware and software that govern the way a user interacts with, and performs the operations on, the system. The software portion of the user interface may contain a Graphical User Interface (GUI) program, a menu-driven program, and an interface program that uses natural language processing techniques.

It is highly desirable that users who are not programmers, system engineers or computer scientists, be able to communicate with the knowledge-base system and get the knowledge and information they need from it. The user interface should have natural language components and not be dependent on having to know a high-level computer language to use the system. A high-level computer language is a programming language whose concepts and structures do not reflect the structure of any computer, and is higher than machine instructions. High-level languages like BASIC and PASCAL are nearer to human than machine instructions, but a computer novice must learn this strict and precise artificial language before he can use the computer.

An expert system should have a natural language interface program that allows users to communicate interactively with a computer via a terminal in English. This type of interface is sometimes called *natural language front end*. A natural language user interface should have some natural language components such as, a taxonomy of concepts, pragmatic grammars, semantics, and a number of special purpose rules for processing various types of sentences. Besides these natural language components, the user interface must have interactive query capability so the users can manipulate the knowledge-base, search the data base, carry out report generating functions, and make recommendations.

Thus, a computer novice or a clerk can compose queries and carry out other search and report functions with little effort instead of having to learn a computer language. The natural language interface also will enable ordinary users to enter a request in English to retrieve information and knowledge stored in the knowledge base. This is different from a typical database query that requires a specific set of commands, structure and format, and that no matching parenthesis is left out before it can be executed. Let us look at the following example:

> Suppose that you were the manager of a Mercedes-Benz Automobiles Service Center, which has a database management system. Also, suppose you want to have a list of available Mercedes-Benz batteries to see if your service center can carry out the recommendations in the production rules, given in example 10 of Chapter 8. Without using relational operations, such as *INTERSECT WITH, FORMING FROM,* AND *SELECT,* you might type your request in the following way:

FIND (MERCEDES-BENZ OR 300E) AND (BATTERIES)

If you make a typing error or forget a parenthesis, your system will not retrieve the desired information. However, if you had a knowledge-based system and a natural language interface, you can process the same request in the following ways:

- *Show me a list of Mercedes-Benz Batteries.*
- *What do you have about Model 300E?*

Some Useful Search Techniques

The user of a knowledge-based system may ask many questions about the data and knowledge that are stored in the computer. The search capability and how long it takes to find what you want, depends on the physical data organization and the addressing techniques employed. Except for mentioning them, we will not discuss them further in this Chapter. However, there are several useful search techniques that you can use on a knowledge-based system or expert system. Some of these search techniques are described below.

Backward Chaining. The first search technique is *backward chaining.* With this technique, the user must try to search backwards from a desired goal and reason backward to the state he would have had to be in at the starting point (the initial state). From this process, the user will use inference procedures through a chain of rules in an attempt to find a verifiable set of condition clauses. This goal-oriented search technique follows a strategy which says that a person always has a good reason for needing a particular fact before trying to determine its value.

Forward Chaining. With this search technique, the user or problem-solver begins the search with given facts or the condition clause of a rule, and works "forward" through a chain of rules in an attempt to activate implied action clauses toward the goal state. Here, the user or problem-solver tries to search forward from given facts or conditions through some set of paths that converge satisfactorily on the goal or goal state.

Heuristic Search. After successfully using various search techniques repeatedly for solutions in large problem spaces, you might want to "prune" some operator sequences or reduce the size of your search space, or even optimize your search with a rule-of-thumb or heuristic approach. This approach may involve using constraints on the overall solution at an early stage of the search to filter the alternatives and reduce the breadth or depth of the search space. It also can include such procedures as *choice-set, step-order, hill climbing, minimax, path test* and others. Remember that this rule-of-thumb approach is not an *algorithmic* approach, and it does not guarantee an optimal search solution. For a *heuristic* search only offers a solution that is good enough most of the time.

Other Important Features of an Expert System

We have thus far described the nature and structure of knowledge-based systems or expert systems. Notwithstanding the fact that these systems vary in design and have their own characteristics, there are certain things we can expect a "good" expert system to do. A good expert system should be able to do the following:

- Normally operate in an on-line question-and-answer dialogue with an ordinary user or client.
- Retrieve data and display the value of an attribute of a specific object.
- Query its knowledge base if it requires an arithmetic process.
- The client or user should be able to use it to help diagnose a problem, and determine its causes.
- The client should be able to ask a *WHY* question, which causes the system to determine the identity of an action and the rules that the system is currently considering.
- The client should be able to ask a *HOW* question, which causes the system to explain how it reached its conclusion. This explanation, in English, would include the rules used to make the conclusion.
- The system should be able to answer questions that were misspelled or about a point that may not be clear to the user.
- And, the system should be able to ask the user questions to gain additional information to solve the problem at hand. It also should manifest machine learning.

Chapter 10 discusses expert system opportunities, and gives a step-by-step guide to expert system development. We suggest that you answer the questions below before proceeding to Chapter 10.

Questions for Discussion and Review

1. What are the main features of an expert system?

2. What are the economic and educational benefits of an expert system?

3. Explain the following terms:

    Domain expert
    Knowledge engineer
    LISP
    PROLOG

4. Describe four types of representational systems that can be used to represent knowledge, events, and generalization.

5. What is the knowledge component of an expert system? What is the function of an inference system (engine) in an expert system?

6. What is a *natural language front end*? How different is a natural language front end from relational operations in a Relational Database.

7. Describe the concepts of backward chaining and forward chaining. What is a heuristic search? Mention few heuristic search procedures in your answer.

Chapter 10

Expert System Opportunities and a Step-by-Step Guide to Expert System Development

The Need for Expert Knowledge

An expert is a person with a high degree of skill in a problem area or knowledge of a certain field of discipline. Experts vary from a distinguished professor of chemistry and Nobel laureate, a professor or expert consultant in infectious diseases, to a systems engineer that configures computer systems to meet varied applications.

Human experts as described above are scarce and are usually in short supply. In some instances, a patient may have to accept less than complete treatment and may die, or a corporation can experience poor asset utilization and a loss of revenue without an expert. In this context, knowledge has extremely high value and is related to efficiency. Knowledge also is clearly a capability that is needed.

Criteria for Domain Experts

A domain expert must be task specific in that he needs to analyze a task or problem and know specific things about the problem in order to solve it. A domain expert must have certain expertise or valuable knowledge that he or she wants to transfer from the human brain or cognition to a computer.

But first, the expert must want to do it willingly like Dr. Jack Myers in the INTERNIST and CADUCEUS Projects. Second, the domain expert must know a great deal about the problem domain and how to solve problems. Although these are necessary conditions for a domain expert, they are not sufficient. A person who can solve a problem, but is unable to explain the result or determine whether his solution is relevant or not to his domain of knowledge will need explanatory skills and a systematic organization of thought to meet our criteria for a domain expert. Third, an expert must be able to explain the result. Fourth, an expert must be able to learn and restructure the knowledge for comprehension. And fifth, the expert must be able to determine whether certain statements are correct, and whether the advice, judgement, and suggested procedure for attempting to solve the problem are relevant.

Expert System Opportunities

Economic progress in a modern society requires knowledge, information, skilled management, and money capital. Knowledge increases the capability of an individual and an organization, and improves productivity. As a social product, knowledge is invaluable. In an emergency, knowledge of the solution to a medical problem or having the correct diagnosis can save lives. The value of human lives is hard to assess.

Some observers believe that in the global scene, in the twenty-first century (year 2001), knowledge will play a decisive role in competitive markets. Edward A. Feigenbaum and Pamela McCorduck (1985), in "The Fifth Generation, Artificial Intelligence and Japan's Computer Challenge to the World" made a spirited argument linking knowledge to Adam Smith's *Inquiry into the Nature and Causes of the Wealth of Nations*. Feigenbaum and McCorduck argued "the new wealth of nations has its source not in land, or in labor, or in capital alone, but in *knowledge*." Feigenbaum and McCorduck also showed how Japan is committed to produce not only a new generation of computers within the next decade, but to establish a "knowledge industry" in which knowledge will be a saleable commodity.

Advances in information technology have brought new opportunities for small institutions and businesses. This generation has experienced a computer revolution that brings changes and opportunities for small colleges and universities, teachers, and businesses. Before this revolution, knowledge based systems (expert systems) were developed and operated on million-dollar mainframes and high-end minicomputers. And, most small institutions and businesses could not afford such expensive computing resources.

But dramatic technological leaps in the capability of micro-processors, storage technology, computer architecture and information technology have brought radical changes to the size, capability, and the cost of computers. Today, there are low cost, high performance personal computers and powerful workstations that small institutions and businesses can buy. Now, they can take advantage of expert system and knowledge processing software, which can run on small and powerful computers that can cost as low as $20,000. For the first time, there is a cost-effective delivery system for knowledge processing and expert system that can be on your desktop. What a powerful tool for the knowledge worker!

These technological developments offer new opportunities for small institutions and businesses. Now they can use expert systems to capture scarce and specialized knowledge and incorporate it in their computer systems. Family doctors and general practitioners can now afford to use an expert system to help diagnose and give therapy for certain diseases. Medical schools can use expert systems as an on-the-job tutor for interns, and small businesses can use expert systems as an aid for sales consultants in situations requiring different configurations.

Steps in Expert System Development

Expert system development takes time and diligence. So, careful planning is necessary. And, before deciding to build an expert system, you need to know which particular problem domain or area of expertise is needed most, or which skill will save lives, or which knowledge has the highest payoff. Then you need to conduct a feasibility study. If management approves and agrees to commit resources to the expert system project, you will need a plan – a way of proceeding – toward the development of an expert system.

There is no rigid scientific formula for the number of steps that must be taken in expert system development, but, there is a general systems approach, which suggests a logical order of steps for developing a wide range of system projects. These steps have been successfully applied over the last thirty years. So, we will use a general systems approach to illustrate our guide to expert system development. The flowchart in *Figure 10-1* shows a graphical representation of a step-by-step guide to expert system development.

Step 1, the Domain Expert. This is a person with expertise in a specific field of knowledge in the domain of the expert system that is being developed. The domain expert works closely with the knowledge engineer to impart the expert knowledge into a knowledge-based system managed by a computer. In step 1, the domain expert defines the problem and describes some typical problem situations.

Step 2, the Knowledge Engineer. This is an Artificial Intelligence (AI) specialist that is responsible for the technical part in developing a knowledge based/expert system. The knowledge engineer works closely with the domain expert to transfer the knowledge of the expert to a computer system. Other duties and responsibilities of the knowledge engineer are described in subsequent steps of the flow chart (See *Figure 10-1*). In step 2, the knowledge engineer writes the problem description and extracts some basic concepts and ideas about the problem, which the expert system is intended to serve.

Step 3, Problem Description. In step 3, the knowledge engineer presents the problem description to the domain expert to see if the description is accurate and fully represents the problem as defined by the domain expert. If not, the domain expert will suggest changes and perhaps give additional examples. The knowledge engineer will revise the description and present it again to the domain expert. If the domain expert is still not yet satisfied, he will suggest further changes. This feedback process will continue until the domain expert is satisfied that the description represents the problem that the expert system is to solve.

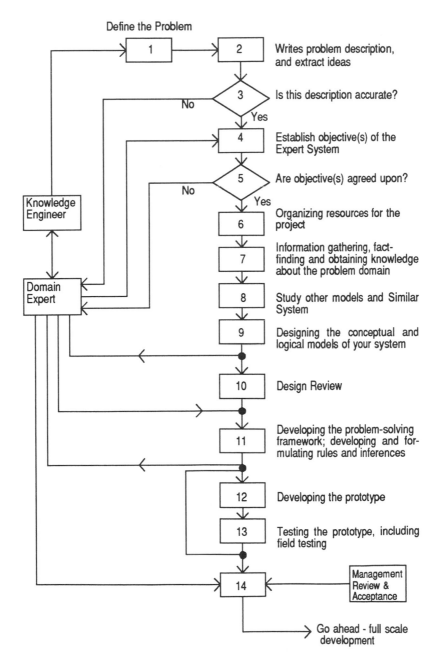

Figure 10-1. Flowchart for Knowledge Based/Expert System Development

Step 4, Establishing the Objectives of the System. In step 4, the knowledge engineer works with the domain expert to establish the objective(s) of the system. The objective is the desired outcome, which the domain expert and knowledge engineer intend to progress towards or obtain at a later time. The statement about the objectives should include the limits of the project and conditions under which the project will be done. It also should include a description of the output to be produced by the expert system.

Step 5, Agreement on the Objectives and Goals of the System. In step 5, there is a condition in the following question, are the objectives agreed upon? If not, the domain expert will suggest changes to the knowledge engineer. The process will continue until the objectives are clearly understood.

Step 6, Organizing the Resources for the Project. The domain expert must be satisfied with the description made by the knowledge engineer. In other words, the description must accurately represent the problem which the expert system is to solve, and the objectives of the expert system must be clearly understood. The next job is to organize the resources for the project.

The knowledge engineer needs to have answers to such questions as: does a single domain expert have all the knowledge necessary for our system? How many technical assistants and programmers are needed? Also, the knowledge engineer or project leader may have to hire consultants or specialists personnel on a short-term basis so the project can be successfully completed within a projected time frame.

Step 7, the Knowledge Engineer Gathers Information and Obtains Knowledge about the Problem Domain. The knowledge engineer should become familiar with the problem domain. He must studiously read college text books, reference books, procedure manuals, articles and other background materials, to understand what the field of knowledge or task is about. Also, he has to get an understanding of the terms and jargons that pervade the field. For having a good understanding of the physiology, and gathering facts, and studiously reading text books, reference books and articles on infectious diseases can help a knowledge engineer become familiar with the problem domain of medicine and infectious diseases.

Step 8, Study Other Models and Similar Systems. For whatever system that will be developed, it is likely that there is a similar type of expert system in use, somewhere in another organization. In this case, the knowledge engineer should visit that site and observe the system at work. If this is not possible, the knowledge engineer should obtain and study all articles, books, and factual reports about the system or other models of expert systems, like MYCIN, INTERNIST, CADUCEUS, DIGITALIS ADVISOR, XCON, TEIRESIAS, and others.

Step 9, Designing the Conceptual and Logical Models. Before we begin to store the knowledge and determine the rules for a knowledge based system, we need to describe as best we can, the foundation of our knowledge based system. This foundation is known as the *conceptual and logical models.* The conceptual model is a communications tool, which is used to organize, visualize, plan and communicate ideas. This plan would contain a list of the objects and classes of objects in the problem domain. Also, we have to determine what facts are important, and what facts about these objects that we can answer questions about. Furthermore, we have to know what kind of relationships exist between the various objects, and what relationship is an object involved in? Normally, a conceptual model would have a network diagram of some kind.

The conceptual model has to be mapped to the logical model. The logical model involves the design of the data structure and flow diagrams containing facts, objects, attributes, data elements, attribute values set, associations, and a logical chain. It is useful to divide the whole problem into subproblems and show the relationships among the various subproblems and objects.

The knowledge engineer may have to take these models to the domain expert for consultation. Particularly, if it is discovered that something was omitted from the original problem description or it is necessary to add another level of detail or refinement to the description on step 2.

Step 10, Design Review. This is the final stage of the logical model of the knowledge based system. The logical schema and the users' view should be examined. The output layout and output techniques should be examined. It should be remembered that the ordinary users of this system will frequently be computer novices. Also, the purpose of the design review is to identify flaws and eliminate modification anolomies.

The review panel should include a representative from the users' group and a member from the enterprise or management group. At the end of the design review, the review panel should produce a list of problems discovered, give approval, and make recommendations on the next step to be taken.

Step 11, Developing the Problem Solving Framework. After approval of the conceptual and logical models, the next stage is to transform the knowledge collected into a particular knowledge-based construct. The knowledge engineer must choose which of several problem-solving frameworks, inference procedures and development techniques best suit the new domain.

It is important that the knowledge engineer be familiar with programming in such languages as C, PROLOG, and LISP. Also, he or she must have knowledge of the following: data structure, various techniques of knowledge representation and heuristic search used in expert system and other intelligent systems, and development tools such as ART (Automated Reasoning Tool), KEE (Knowledge Engineering Environment), KES (Knowledge Engineering System) and others.

Besides the technical requirements for a knowledge engineer, the person must be able to persuade the domain expert to participate and cooperate fully. The person (the knowledge engineer) must be able to listen intensely and evaluate the various methods of knowledge representation and inferences that match the expert's behavior.

The knowledge engineer also must work with his team to develop a set of rules to represent the knowledge communicated by the domain expert. The knowledge engineer must work closely with the domain expert to make sure that the set of rules being developed is adequate for solving the problem and objectives described in step 3 and 4. The knowledge engineer will test these rules and expand them. The knowledge engineer also must find rules for exceptions.

The development process takes time and diligence. There is a series of actions, changes and functions that have to be carried out, and delays can occur. However, the knowledge engineer can employ a set of expert system development tools to improve the efficiency of the development process, and allow a prototype to be developed rapidly.

Step 12, Developing the Prototype. At this stage, the logical schema and formalized rules and inferences are programmed into the computer that has been chosen for the system development, so a transformation process can take place. The logical model coupled with the formalized rules and inferences are then transformed into constructs, which are available within the particular model of the expert system development tools. The first-form prototype derived from this transformation will serve as the model for a larger system. This "first-form" model is a suitable representation of the design of the expert system.

Step 13, Testing the Prototype. At this stage, the computer hardware and peripherals are installed and tested; programs are coded, debugged and tested, knowledge rules and inferences are converted, procedures are documented, and the prototype is up and running. The knowledge engineer must work with the domain expert to test the prototype to see if the rules were implemented correctly, to see if there is any weakness in the structure of the system, to make sure that the premise does not contain any clauses that will fail in the context in which it will be used, to check for any inconsistency, and to make sure that the prototype can provide valid solutions to a problem domain just as those of the human expert; that is, the use of real problems as part of the field test.

Close interaction between the knowledge engineer and the domain expert allows corrections, adjustments, revisions, and fine tuning of the prototype to take place efficiently. The knowledge engineer also must work with user groups and pay attention to the user interface. The user interface may include both hardware and software that allow nontechnical users to interact with and perform operations on the expert system. There should be a thorough field testing of the prototype. The expert system should be easy to use.

Step 14, the Acceptance Stage. After all the problems, errors and revisions have been completed satisfactorily, the prototype should be presented to management and users of the system for acceptance. The acceptance stage should include a presentation of the prototype in a nontechnical seminar or session. The presenters should explain how the system works, how easy it is to use, and how well it performs in "real life" situations. The prototype should demonstrate how a knowledge-based system or expert system works to a wide-ranging audience that might include an expert who wants to query its knowledge base, a user who requested its services, and a student with minimal experience of the problem domain who wants to learn from it.

Questions and answers should be encouraged, and a schedule for training users of the system should be established. After the prototype is accepted, management will give the development team permission to proceed with the project and its implementation.

Balancing Euphoria with Reality – A Paradigm for the Human Expert

The euphoria about the future of computers and computer-based expert system is understandable. But, we must be certain to balance that euphoria with reality. For it is important to understand that not all problems are easily reduced into axioms or production rules. Some problems are complex and require imagination, resourcefulness, intuition and inductive reasoning. These properties are found only in the human expert.

Thoughtful observers of modern science have always been struck by intuition, and the inductive character of excellent scientists or experts. The nature of inductive logic has been considered by a long list of notable thinkers including Bacon, Mills, Venn, Jevons and others. I am not going to thrust into an analysis of the process of induction. Rather, I want to consider here intuition and other properties in the organization of thought that are found in the human expert and not in any artifact or computer system. These properties are required to solve complex and multifaceted problems.

The human expert uses imagination, intuition, and resourcefulness that are properties of perception. How does science or technology account for the mental leaps of human knowledge? Moreover, when a human expert is faced with an unexpected situation, he makes mental leaps over inference that later becomes coherent with experience at hindsight.

When we think of a human expert, we often think of a person with a high degree of skill in or knowledge of a certain subject. We think of an expert as a person who has demonstrated impressive skill, dexterity, resourceful and quick thinking under pressure, original, and ingenious.

If you observe the human expert at work, you will notice that the human expert can handle novel and unexpected situations, and sometimes, with quick-thinking under pressure. For the ability to handle unique and unexpected situations successfully, is often what cause the person to be judged as an expert.

In contrast, an artificial expert system handles the typical cases or standard problems that human experts have accumulated after dealing with similar situations. A computer based expert (system) can store a list of the most common problems, possible causes, and can give the user a guide to a solution. But, when it comes to complex problems, malfunctions and the unexpected situations, you have to refer the case or problems to a human expert. Therefore, I assert that an artificial expert (system) is an aid or a knowledge tool, and not an expert on the grounds that the real expert uses more than logical and *heuristic* methods to solve problems.

Knowledge Synergy

Further, a human expert can combine his expertise with an expert system and push the field of knowledge to its boundary. This combination of human expert with expert-system tool can increase the performance of the human expert and lead to better learning curve. When the combine performance is greater than the sum of its parts, the measure of the joint effects is called *synergy*. *Knowledge synergy* will increase the degree of knowledge and understanding of the field of knowledge. This area is one of enormous potential that needs further inquiry in the future.

Questions for Discussion and Review

1. What are the criteria for a domain expert?

2. What are the functions and characteristics of a knowledge engineer?

3. Describe three successful knowledge-based (expert) systems.

4. How can an expert system help a small institution or business?

5. Advances in computer technology have removed certain constraints that prevented individuals and professionals who did not have access to mainframe computers to use or develop expert systems. Discuss these changes and show how these changes can create new opportunities for the professional or a small establishment.

6. What is the advantage of using an expert system development tool? Describe briefly two expert system development tools.

7. How can a computer-based expert system help the human expert?

8. What is *knowledge synergy*, and how can knowledge synergy increase the degree of understanding in a domain of knowledge?

9. Explain the role of the conceptual and logical models in the design of an expert system.

10. What is meant by the term rapid prototype? What is the goal of a prototype in expert system development?

Chapter 11

Epilogue, or The Road Ahead – The 21st Century

In the ten preceding Chapters, we discussed the basics of a computer system and showed how computers have evolved from a computation machine to a tool that will have a significant impact on nearly every aspect of higher education. We have shown how the computer can capture expert knowledge, store knowledge, make decisions, make diagnoses and with communications technology can easily replicate and distribute knowledge across boundaries. Computer and communications technology are developing so rapidly that the consequences of ignoring or underestimating the impact of these technologies on training, teaching and learning, and on higher education are fatal.

In this book, we argued and showed how computers can augment the traditional teaching methods, how computers can help in remedial education, and how computers and information technology can improve the delivery and distribution of knowledge and education. Yet, we have never promised that the computer and information technology is the panacea to the goals of meeting all of tomorrow's challenges.

As we move toward the dawn of the 21st century, there are some serious challenges facing higher education and our society. These challenges while involving knowledge, computers, and information technology, cover a wider scope than the topic of this book. However, in this epilogue, we will explore the scope of the challenges and the way in which these challenges can affect higher education in the years ahead.

The Scope of the Challenges

Less Public Funding

The world of higher education is changing dramatically. The periods of great expansion and the days when resources and public funding from State, Federal and Local Governments were plentiful are gone.

When the Government begins to find the financial road difficult, it will cut back first in student support and then on funds to universities. Economic forecasts show that the percentage of Government funding will decline further. Meanwhile, there are many diverse student bodies and a wide range of competing constituencies all competing for scarce and dwindling resources; yet there are more changes and challenges to come. There is also uncertainty in the amount of revenue from Federal and State appropriations for colleges and universities.

International Economic Development

On the international scene, newly industrialized countries in Asia (such as Japan, Singapore and others) that are impatient to reach the economic level of more advanced countries are competing successfully in the industrial, commercial and consumer goods markets. But the overwhelming majority of nations of the world still have elementary or less developed economies, and are yearning for knowledge. Besides these developments, was the collapse of the Soviet Union, with the result that many communist countries of Eastern and Central Europe including Russia are trying to make a successful post-communist transformation into market economies. Such a transformation would include the restructuring of their higher education institutions, and possibly the knowledge in such fields of discipline as economics, education, law, medicine, engineering, and management. Finally, there is South Africa, a country with enormous resources emerging from an *apartheid* policy (an official policy of racial segregation) to democratic reform, and a full reintegration with the world economy.

As you can see, the world of economics and politics is different from the past. Newly industrialized nations are competing successfully for markets and less developed countries are offering overseas investors attractive incentives including tax exemptions and low cost labor to lure foreign investors into offshore manufacturing in their countries.

Rising Cost of College Education and Falling Standards

The cost of college education is rising steadily. As an example, in 1993 - 1994 the average cost at a public college in the U.S.A. was approximately $8,600 and $18,000 at private colleges. These costs do not include other costs such as commuting, traffic congestion, expensive parking fees, the high stress of the commute, and often many other costs such as the case when students have to travel to another college within the system to get the right classes to graduate.

Although some colleges and universities are doing a good job, parents, industry and community leaders believe that many colleges and universities are not providing students with the proper knowledge, level of skills, and understanding of ethical standards and values in a healthy society. Their programs are being questioned as well. Besides the general education requirements of a modern society, the student should acquire some skills that will enable him or her to carry out some useful function of society or at least be "employable."

Technology

Technology, the application of science to industry, commerce or organization is an important ingredient of economic growth. The computer and information technology have permeated our lives and reached beyond disciplinary boundaries. In the previous Chapters, we have seen how computers have emerged from a computation machine to data processing, then to information processing, and finally to knowledge processing where computers are experts and follow reasoning.

After the collapse of the Soviet Union and the end of the *cold war* – the state of rivalry between the Soviet Union and Western Bloc, following World War II – the United States Government has been encouraging various Defence Agencies and Contractors to transfer their knowledge, techniques and technology to the civilian economy. Some of the applied sciences such as cybernetics, system engineering and management science that were used successfully in many defence and aerospace projects are definitely transferable to higher education.

Management

One of the most serious problems facing higher education today is management. Notice that I use the word management instead of "administration," which connotes administering the affairs of an institution or the executive branch of government or the tendering of something such as an oat, sacrament or medicine. Although the words "management" and "administration" are sometimes used interchangeably, to me "management" is the act, manner or practice of managing, handling or controlling the use of (a tool, system, a weapon or) resources.

This management concept should start from the selection of a President then the provost/vice president of academic affairs and other upper levels. The selection committee must understand what skills, experience and characteristics are required to manage a modern university or college. Some universities are moving toward a management concept but at the community college level, many administrators are aloof, inert and oblivious of the changes that are taking place. Serious and urgent reform is needed in this sector of higher education.

Cybernetics and System Concepts

An important challenge to higher education administration is its awareness. In the last fifty years, cyberneticians and systems engineers have developed and articulated the importance of an awareness of the interactions between the parts of a system and the system within its environment. A system must be *adaptive* when there is a deep change in its environment else it becomes inefficient and does not perform its functions properly. Another relevant concept is homeostasis. *Homeostasis* is the tendency for the internal environment of the body to reach an equilibrium state it seeks to maintain in response to environmental changes.

Strategic Planning

As we move into the 21st century, colleges and universities should be more enterprising. Most of the assumptions made on long-range plans for many campuses across the nation no longer apply. As profound changes are occurring rapidly internationally and in the nation. These changes require the modern college or university to respond, adapt, and progress in ways that allow the system to meet commitments to future students in providing the highest quality education in an cra of greatly reduced public funding.

The President and his or her vice-presidents must adopt strategic planning concepts, productivity improvements, and develop information system models beyond the CAMPUS model. The CAMPUS (Comprehensive Analytical Methods of Planning in University Systems) Model has its origin in the work, "A New Tool for Education Administrations," a simulation in higher education by R.W. Judy, and J.B. Levine in 1965. It is a very useful analytical tool and can answer questions on resource implications of changes in staffing, curriculum, and admissions.

A strategic planning framework is described in Anthony's "Planning and Control System." In that volume, Anthony describes strategic planning as "the process of deciding on objectives of the organization, on changes in these objectives, on the resources used to attain these objectives, and on the policies that are to govern the acquisition, use, and disposition of these resources." A strategic planning framework must include non-academic personnel, support services, costing and budgets.

Also, we must be able to predict enrollment at the undergraduate freshmen level, the Community College transfer level, and graduate enrollment level, professional school level. And, we must relate enrollments to manpower requirements to meet changes.

Social Function

The university has a social role to play nationally and internationally. Nationally, it must improve its relations with Latinos, Blacks and other under represented minorities. For it should be understood that perceived inequality and alienation can serve as a breeding ground of intolerance of one kind or another. The university will face this challenge and must strive to maintain social respect and academic excellence, otherwise, it would not be relevant in the eyes of everyone - the rich or the poor, men and women, middle-class whites or low income minorities.

In this age of global communications and markets, the university or college should play a role. They can attract good quality of students from overseas, and promote better understanding of different cultures and institutions.

Information Technology and Distance Learning

Finally, there should be an information technology strategy. This does not mean a plan to buy whatever is new or cheap. The information technology strategy should define the technological role as applied to the overall strategic planning and the conduct of the operations of the college or university.

Traditional colleges and universities should not make the mistake of dismissing an Education Network System and distance learning. The technology is here and people are concerned with the rising costs of traditional education, commuting, traffic congestion, expensive parking fees, and stress. In addition, to what was described in Chapter 6, *Computers in Education* of this book, current developments in communications technology give distance learning improved capability and thus, a viable alternative to the conventional lecture method. For example, we can have an information network that allows an instructor or set of instructors to reach larger numbers of students located at local study centers around a geographical region, or State or across States, simultaneously and economically. New technology allows interactive and live communication with voice, video, data and storage capability. Such a network would include a microphone equipped with a response terminal that allows each student to ask questions and answer quizzes. It would allow the instructors to maintain direct video and audio contact, exchange data and monitor results.

This interactive capability between students and instructors represents an improvement in distance learning and in some cases provide better quality of instructions and interaction than traditional education with large auditoriums filled with students, or teaching assistants that are a couple of years older than a freshman, or teaching assistants that cannot communicate clearly. A simple diagram of an Education Network for the 21st Century is depicted on the front cover of this book.

At the dawn of the 21st century, the technology will be in place to permit distance learning systems to reach a new dimension of higher education and training. Let us hope that the people who meet these challenges will have the wisdom, management skills, and moral energy to get their organizations to adapt to the deep changes in the global environment and improve the quality of higher education and the human condition.

Bibliography

Ashby, R.W., *Design for a Brain*, Chapman and Hall, London 1960.

Barr, Avron, and Feigenbaum, Edward A., *The Handbook of Artificial Intelligence, 3 vols.*, William Kaufman, 1981-1982.

Beer S., *The Brain of the Firm.* Allen Lane, The Penguin Press, 1972.

Boole, G., *Mathematical Analysis of Logic*, Oxford, 1948.

Bruner, Jorome S., Oliver, R.R., Greenfield, A.M., et al, *Studies in Cognitive Growth*, John Wiley & Sons, 1966.

Buchanan, Bruce G., and Edward H. Shortliffe, *Rule-Based Expert Programs: The MYCIN Experiments of the Stanford Heuristic Programming Project*, Addison-Wesley, Reading, MA, 1984.

Davis, Randall, and Douglas B. Lenat, *Knowledge-Based Systems in Artificial Intelligence*, McGrow-Hill Book Company, New York, 1982.

DeMorgan, A., *Formal Logic*, edited by Taylor, London, 1926.

Feigenbaum, Edward A., and **Pamela McCorduck**, *The Fifth Generation*, Addison-Wesley, Reading, MA, 1985.

Forrester, J.W., *Industrial Dynamics*, M.I.T. Press, 1961.

George, F.H., *The Brain as a Computer*, Pergamon Press, 1961.

Hirst, P.H. and Peters, R.S., *The Logic of Education*, London: Routledge, 1970.

Judy, R.W. and Levine, J.B., *A New Tool for Educational Administrators (CAMPUS)*, University of Toronto, 1965.

Katz, D., MacCoby and Morse, N.C., *Productivity, Supervision, and Morale in an Office Situation,* Survey Research Center, Institute for Social Research, University of Michigan, December, 1950.

Lorimer, Kenneth V., "A Cybernetics and Education." Monograph. Cybernetics and Information Technology Centre, CA 1985.

Lorimer, Kenneth V., "Do We Need a New Types of MBA Graduate?" *America Business Today,* Vol.1 No.1.

Lorimer, Kenneth V., *A Cybernetic Approach to the Design of Management Information Systems,* Brunel University, Uxbridge, England, 1974.

Lorimer Kenneth V., *Higher Education System and Their Functions,* Link-Frame Publishing International 1996.

McCarthy J., "First Order Theories of Individual Concepts and Propositions," *Machine Intelligence,* Ellis Horwood, Vol. 9, 1979.

McCulloch, W.S., and Pitts, W., "A Logical Calculus of Ideas Imminent in Nervous Activity," *Bull Math. Biophysics,* Vol. 5, 1943.

McDermott, John, "R1: A Rule-Based Configurer of Computer Systems," *Artificial Intelligence,* Vol. 19, No.1, 1982.

Miller, G.A., Galanter, and Pribram, K.H., *Plans and the Structure of Behavior,* Holt Dryden, New York, 1971.

Newell, A., and Simmon, H.A., *Human Problem Solving,* Prentice-Hall, Englewood Cliffs, N.J., 1972.

Newell A., Shaw, J.C. and Simmon, H.A., "Report on a General Problem-Solving Program for a Computer," *Proceedings of the International Conference on Information Processing,* UNESCO, Paris, 1960.

Newell, A., and Simon, H.A., "The Logic Theory Machine," *IRE Transactions on Information Theory,"* Vol. 1F2, No.3, 1956.

Pask, G. and Scott, B.C., *"CASTE: A System for Exhibiting Learning Strategies and Regulating Uncertainties,"* Systems Research, Survey, 1973.

Piaget, J., *The Origin of Intelligence in the Child*, Penguin Books Ltd., 1977.

Pople, Harry E., Jr., "Heuristic Methods for Imposing Structure on Ill-Structured Problems; The Structuring of Medical Diagnostics," in *Artificial Intelligence in Medicine*, edited by Peter Szolovits, Westview Press, Boulder, CO, 1982.

Rosenblueth A., Wiener, N. and Bigelow, J., "Behavior Purpose and Teleology." *Philosophy of Science,* Baltimore, January, 1943.

Russell, Bertrand, *Education and the Social Order*, UNWIN Books, 1971.

Schultz, Theodore, *The Economic Value of Education*, Columbia University Press, 1963.

Shannon, C. and Weaver, W., *The Mathematical Theory of Communication*, University of Illinois Press, Urbana, Chicago.

Sherwood, Bruce Arne, *The Tutor Language*, (for PLATO), Control Data Education Company, 1977.

Skinner, B.F., "Teaching Machines," *Science*, 1958.

Temple, Baker & Sloane Inc., *The Benefits of the Graphical User Interface*, Microsoft and Zenith Data Systems, 1990.

Turing, A.M., "On Computable Numbers with an Application to the Entscheidungsproblem," *Proc. Lond. Math. Soc.* (2), 42, 230.

Weiner, N., *Cybernetics: or Control and Communication in the Animal and the Machine*, Cambridge Massachusetts.

Whitehead, A.N., and Russell, B.A., *Principia Mathematica,* Vol. 1, Cambridge, 1910.

Zadeh, L.A., "Outline of a New Approach to the Analysis of Complex Systems and Decision Process." *IEE Transactions on Systems, Man and Cybernetics.* Vol. SMC-3, No. 1, January, 1973.

Trademarks

Apple, Macintosh and Lisa are trademarks of Apple Computer Corporation, Inc.

ART is trademark of Inference Corporation.

COMPAQ is a registered trademark of COMPAQ Corporation.

CP/M is registered trademark of the Digital Research Inc.

dBASE is a trademark of Ashton-Tate.

DEC is a registered trademark of Digital Equipment Corporation.

IBM, IBM PC, IBM PC/XT, IBM-AT are trademarks of International Business Machines, Inc.

Intel Processors, and the Pentium Processor are trademarks of Intel Corporation.

KEE or Knowledge Engineering Environment is a registered trademark of IntelliCorp.

Lotus 1-2-3 is a registered trademark of Lotus Development Corporation.

Microsoft, MS-DOS, Windows, Windows 95, and Windows NT are trademarks of Microsoft Corporation.

OS/2 is a trademark of International Business Machine.

Sea World

UNIX is a trademark of Bell Laboratories.

WordPerfect is registered trademark of the WordPerfect Corporation.

Z80 is trademark of Zilog, Inc.

ZipDrive is a trademark of IOMEGA.

Index

Q

Book Order Form

You can order this book from your local bookstore or order directly from the Publisher. You can copy this convenient order form, and use it for ordering.

Name:_____

Company/Institution:_____

Address:_____

_____

Qty	Title	ISBN	Unit Price	Total
	Education, Knowledge and the Computer	0-9647688-0-1	$29.95	

Subtotal:	
CA Residents 7% Tax:	
Shipping & Handling:	$4.00
Total (US Dollars):	

* Canada and Overseas: If you want your order shipped Air or Express Delivery, please state this when ordering. The additional charges will be added to your bill.

Ship to: (if address is different from the above)

_____

_____

_____ Payment enclosed (Check or Money Order)
      (Make check payable to **Link-Frame Publishing International**)

Charge my: _____VISA _____Mastercard _____Discover Card

Card Expiration Date:_____

Credit Card #: _____

Signature:_____

      Mail your book order to: Link-Frame Publishing International
                                P.O. Box 26265
                                San Diego, CA 92196
                                U.S.A.
                                Tel: (619)566-9664

For Faster Service FAX: (619)566-5485